NATURAL
CREATIVITY

DAYBREAK: 52 Things Nature Teaches Us

*Natural Acts: Reconnecting with Nature to
Recover Community, Spirit, and Self*

NATURAL CREATIVITY

Exploring and Using Nature's Raw Materials to Craft Simple, Functional, and Attractive Objects

Amy E. Dean

with illustrations by the author

M Evans
Lanham • New York • Boulder • Toronto • Plymouth, UK

M Evans
An imprint of Rowman & Littlefield
4501 Forbes Boulevard, Suite 200
Lanham, Maryland 20706
www.rowman.com

10 Thornbury Road, Plymouth PL6 7PP
United Kingdom

M. Evans and Company, Inc.
216 East 49th Street
New York, New York 10017

Library of Congress Cataloging-in-Publication Data

Dean, Amy.
Natural creativity : exploring and using nature's raw materials to craft simple, functional, and attractive objects / Amy E. Dean.
p. cm.
Includes bibliographical references.
ISBN 978-0-87131-852-7
1. Nature craft—United States. 2. Handicraft—United States—History. 3. Nature study—United States—Activity programs. I. Title.
TT157.D384   1998   745.5—dc21   98-4716

Book design and type formatting by Bernard Schleifer

Manufactured in the United States of America

First Edition

Distributed by
NATIONAL BOOK NETWORK

*To Uncle B., the family woodcrafter,
and my cousin, Chris, who every Christmas
touches me with her gift of creativity.*

A pile of rocks ceases to be a pile of rocks when somebody contemplates it with the idea of a cathedral in mind.

— ANTOINE DE SAINT-EXUPERY

Contents

Introduction

On Thursday, September 28, 1995, one of the best-loved specimen trees at the Arnold Arboretum in Boston—an old **Amur cork tree** that had lived for 121 years—died. Its low, spreading limbs had, for years, lured both adults and children to come near it, to touch its bark so much that the normally rough surface was rubbed to a smooth polish. It had enticed Arboretum visitors to climb up onto its low branches for picture-perfect poses in its ancient and proud embrace.

But the magnetism of the tree is what eventually killed it. The steady parade of people to the tree had compacted the soil around its base, smothering its roots, and the endless stream of climbers on its beckoning branches had taken its toll. One day, when a group of twenty-two children were perched together on a limb, the majestic tree cracked audibly and partially uprooted. The most pho-tographed—and the most loved—tree in the arboretum was dead.

Amur Cork Tree. Broadleaf, leaves alternate, aromatic fruits ripen from green to black

Two years later, *Boston Globe* writer Richard Higgins took his five-year-old daughter Emily to the arbore-tum for a ride on her bike. When he asked her where in the park she would like to ride, she replied, "The treehouse, Daddy." What treehouse could she possibly mean? Higgins wondered. The arboretum's rules did not allow for the construction of any treehouse, and he could not recall ever seeing anything in the park that even remotely suggested a treehouse. But, as Emily told him more about the special treehouse she wanted to visit, Higgins suddenly realized that his daughter was referring to what remained of the beloved cork tree—a twenty-foot section of the trunk that lay horizontally over two four-foot stumps. The semblance to a balance beam had not been lost on passersby, particularly the children who would patiently wait in line for the brief pleasure of walking under the limb, balancing their way along it, or jumping off of it. "Even in death," wrote Higgins after his outing with Emily that day, "the tree is magnetic. Emily was all smiles. It was a joy to see her so happy, so vibrant. Such energy, I thought. Such simple love of life. And such an amazing tree!" What Emily and the countless other children in the arboretum saw was not a magnificent tree that had been lost but a really neat play apparatus that had been gained—a play apparatus that had been created both from the natural position of the tree as it lay in repose and the children's own imagination.

To the director of living collections for the arboretum, who composed a powerful testimony to the tree on a memorial plaque that has been placed near the stump of the tree, the tree is history. But to the children who visit the tree each day, the tree is still vital and vibrant, reborn into a new life, resuscitated by the children's delirious shouts of joy and laughter. To the children, the tree is just as wonderful as it was before; it is just different. The fact that the children can create something wonderful out of what adults view as a sad demise is not unusual. For children are blessed from birth with the gift of innocent curiosity-wonder—the ability to ponder as well as to admire. Children can easily make something fun, exciting, interesting, challenging, beautiful, and admirable out of very little. Give a child a popsicle stick and a lump of clay, for example, and minutes later something ingenious will have been created. The dead cork tree can thus become a variety of interesting things to the children—a treehouse, a balance beam, a plank on a pirate's ship, a bridge across a dangerous chasm—because, with each visit, the children let their sense of curiosity-wonder go wild in order to discover and to create.

❦

Creativity is really nothing more than awareness: the ability to notice, to pay attention, to observe, to perceive, to examine, to probe, to consider, to weigh, to appraise, to study, to look, to heed. Such awareness is innate in children. They are, until old enough to be sent to school, mobile little questioning machines that unfailingly notice everything. Awestruck by the world they have entered, their incessant desire to know, to learn, and to understand every little thing can often drive a parent, relative, or caretaker crazy. Like a prosecutor hot for a conviction, children's staccato examination of all things great and small can come across as an endless barrage of unanswerable, unimportant, and even annoying questions: How far can you go down into the ground? What does red taste like? What songs do birds sing? What does an acorn taste like to a **squirrel**? Does sand ever get thirsty? What does the wind feel? Why does chocolate taste so good? While the actual answers to such ques-

Grey Squirrel.

tions are not always critical to children, such innocent questioning provides an instructive and fascinating look into the development of creativity in young minds. For a child's sense of curiosity and wonder shows not just an awareness or even an appreciation of all that is happening in the child's environment but a real reverence for natural life—the air, water, rocks, dirt, grasses, leaves, flowers, bees, trees, birds, the change of seasons, the sun, the moon, and the stars—because such things are vibrant, lively, fascinating, and part of a child's everyday life. Fill a children's museum with space capsules, laser shows, bubble-making machines, mummies, gigantic puzzles, and futuristic computer technology, and set aside a small area in which chicks can be observed as they hatch from their eggs, and the chick exhibit will always be mobbed. Offer a child a store-bought metal whistle or one that has been whittled out of wood, and the child will inevitably choose the woodcrafted whistle. Or, better still, show a child how to make a grass whistle, and the child will not only forever associate wide blades of green grass with sound, but will then explore the musical potential of other greenery. A big part of creativity is discovery, and the natural world is one big treasure hunt to children, full of potential, possibility, and priceless possessions.

Of course once children attend school, they are taught that discovery takes place in classrooms and libraries and learning comes from books and atlases. They are told that their most intriguing questions have no relevance to real life; only one-answer questions are acceptable. So children quickly learn how to supply the one right answer for every "real life" question: What is the capital of Massachusetts? The capital of Massachusetts is Boston. What is 12 divided by 4? Twelve divided by 4 is 3. Who was the first president of the United States? The first president of the United States was George Washington. Any creative talents a child can hold onto as he or she matures—writing, drawing, acting, painting, composing, designing, inventing, exploring, and so on—are considered pasttimes, hobbies, or things done just to pass the time. Rare is the person who, as an adult, can maintain strong links to the creative freedom once granted by childhood wonder and discovery. Instead, adulthood creative energy is shackled to the past—to the same ways of thinking and doing things that others have done before; replicated through mimicry of theme, content, construction, design, format, and so on; or regulated by guidelines, steps, or desired results.

How can you, as an adult, rediscover your awareness, appreciation, and reverence for every little thing in life—for all the things that share the earth with you but which you no longer notice unless they call attention to themselves, such as a moose that lumbers down the main thoroughfare in your town or dandelions that continue to spring up on your lawn despite your assaults on them? To recapture some of your childhood sense of curiosity-wonder about the natural world, you need to first let go of your adult capacity for reasoning. That means that you need to be able to look through a telescope at a starry night sky, for example, and simply notice and appreciate the brightness and colors of the stars rather than try to identify faint galaxies and nebulae or analyze the differences in appearance of Jupiter's bands. As well, you need to release your desire for outcomes—goals; achievements; "right" answers or ways of doing things; or polished, finished products. Then, you can explore ways to exercise your *natural creativity*, or your ability to integrate your own creativity and ingenuity with nature.

This is not as hard to do as you might think, for while your mind may reside in the twentieth century, you are a member of a species that has evolved over time. You still have within you primal instincts; instincts that can emerge when you give them a chance. Such primal instincts involve exploration and discovery of the natural world and its bounties. They are the instincts that once enabled America's earliest settlers to live by their wits and, in so doing, to not just survive in an untamed and rugged wilderness but to live, and live well. The Indians of North America, the early explorers of the continent, and the American colonists all understood that food, water, shelter, clothing, and warmth—the essentials of survival—were readily available and free of charge in the great outdoors. For thousands of years, these people crafted and created practical objects such as birchbark containers, **snowshoes**, and blankets. They grew and harvested nutritious and fortifying crops of corn, beans, and

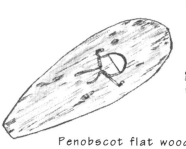

Penobscot flat wooden
snowshoe, with toe hole

squash. They built and maintained protective and snug family shelters. They tracked and hunted animals as well as fished. They designed ingenious and effective weapons and tools such as bows and arrows, knives, and dugout canoes. They fashioned clothing from hides. They designed toys from the leftovers of their gatherings, such as **dolls** made out of cornhusks and dice created from animal bones.

cattail
doll

And so, too, can you. Wilderness materials are still there for the collecting. All you need to have is a willingness to join in spirit with your creative ancestors, and you are on your way to uncovering your potential for natural creativity by making simple, functional, and attractive objects for yourself, your household, or for gift-giving. This book is intended to provide you with both the inspiration and the motivation to create your own crafts from nature's easily collectible raw materials. Because the emphasis is on what you can make out of the materials you are able to gather in locales near you, there are no presentations of finished products or set lists of materials needed for particular projects. Sometimes the steps necessary to craft an object will be provided, as will rough sketches, but because each natural raw material has its own unique shape, color, and texture, what you end up creating will truly be one of a kind. Remember, the point is not for you to make something that someone else has made or that ends up looking a certain way, but for you to *explore the possibilities of your own creative potential* so you can add your own touches of creativity and ingenuity.

This book desires to get you out into nature—to raise your awareness of nature and the natural wonders around you by encouraging you to take a walk on a beach, to hike through a forest, to stroll across a field, to wade in a stream, or to closely examine the herbs and flowers that are growing in your own garden to see what you can find. Natural creativity thus is integral both to the creative process as well as to your physical well-being; natural creativity exercises your mind as well as your body!

How to Use This Book

You may simply enjoy reading this book from cover to cover. Hopefully, it will be a good read and will, at the same time, raise your awareness about America's early settlers, your own ancestral heritage, nature's wonderful array of raw materials, and your connection to "living history"—to the experience of creating and enjoying traditional American crafts.

You may, as well, use this book to guide you on a journey down the path of creative exploration. Find out more about your natural surroundings as well as your own natural creativity by trying one or more of the simple and easy-to-accomplish exercises that are described at the end of each chapter. Or, if you feel up to a natural creativity challenge, accept one or more of the various challenges scattered throughout the book. Each of these challenges are considered to be big projects, which means that there may be numerous steps or instructions to follow and that work on the project may be time consuming. For these challenges, you'll not only need to get outdoors to search for specific natural materials, but you may also need to make or improvise your own tools: remember, battery-operated or electric tools are not acceptable! The challenges oftentimes require a great deal of patience, diligence, and, sometimes, a helping hand or two. Invite your partner, a couple of friends, or even your entire family to participate in any or all of the challenges with you. You may find that sharing in this natural creativity challenge can be beneficial both to your relationship and to your development of a community spirit.

Saguaro Cactus.

1

WILD WISDOM:
Ancestral History of Natural Creativity

To the casual observer, *kapa, Chilkat, kachina, colcha, concha, bulto, mukluk, retablo, santo, Scherenschnitte,* and *jerga* may not sound American, but they are. Most evolved from need: at first, the need to survive; later a need to make useful things beautiful; and in more recent years, the need to preserve tradition as well as to make or own a handmade object in a predominantly mass-produced world. The knowledge to create traditional American crafts, passed from one generation to the next, continues to enrich lives and communities, culturally, environmentally *and* economically. Small wonder that the word *craft,* rooted in the Teutonic *kraft,* originally meant "strength and power."
        —BETSEY B. CREEKMORE, from *Traditional American Crafts: A Practical Guide to 300 Years of Methods and Materials*

WHO ARE THE best traditional craftspeople in America? That's the question that author Betsey B. Creekmore sought to answer as she compiled her book of American crafts and craftsmakers. What she discovered in her search went beyond the reputation and skills of countless craftsmakers, each of whom was nominated by directors and curators of museums, guilds, tribal museums, the Smithsonian Institution, the American Folklife Center at the Library of Congress, national and state art councils, educators, collectors, artisans, and editors of craft publications. Because the true significance of traditional American crafts lies in their origin—in their historic, cultural, and oftentimes ethnic context—as well as in the materials and methods used in creating the crafts, the author based her criteria for a craftsperson's inclusion in the book on two items. First, each craftsperson had to create a craft by adhering to traditional ways, even if that meant that a broom maker had to grow her own broomcorn or a furniture maker had to use only those tools that were available at the time when his furniture was originally constructed. And, second, each craftsperson had to display an understanding of the historic and cultural essence of a craft by knowing the vital role that craft played in the lives of those who used it. With such guidelines in mind, traditional American craftspeople, as defined by Creekmore in her book, were those who ". . . continued to search for: greater perfection within the parameters of their traditions; better methods, tools and finishes; historic details that would further unlock secrets of the past; and ways to pass on what they learned through apprenticeship programs, community education, and publishing."

Traditional American crafts are those objects that were originally created for the survival of this country's early inhabitants and settlers. Because of this, the materials used and the style and manner in which a craft was made tell a great deal about the history of the people as well as the times and conditions in early America. For example, the arrow points that were fashioned by the Indians who once lived in the New England area were made by chipping and flaking flint, jasper, felsite, quartzite, and quartz—the types of stones that were plentiful in the area because of the great quarries that were carved out centuries earlier by glacial activity. However, those Indians who lived in different locales, where such stones may have been scarce, had to craft their own effective **arrow points** out of materials that were available in their particular region of the country, such as animal bones (deer antlers and shank bones were favored) as well as horseshoe crab tails, eagle claws, and, in later years, metals such as brass, copper, and iron.

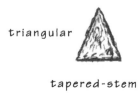
triangular

leaf

tapered-stem

Ancestral Natural Creativity Challenge:

ARROW POINTS

You can make your own arrow point—your own replica of a traditional Indian craft—as the Indians once did out of

- a stone that chips well;
- a large, flat-topped stone that will serve as your anvil, or work area;
- a chipping stone, also called a hammerstone, which needs to be harder than the stone it will chip; and
- a pressure chipper, or a piece of bone (or metal) with a small, rounded end.

Because the chipping stone is your work tool, you need to select a relatively smooth stone that will be comfortable to grip in your hand. It should rest securely against the palm of one hand as you work on your arrow point stone. After you have collected all of your stones, follow these steps:

1. Wear safety glasses to protect your eyes from chips. *This is extremely important!*

2. Position the stone you wish to chip (your arrow point stone) on your anvil.

3. Strike your arrow point stone with your hammerstone sharply at a right angle to the area where you wish to create a fracture. Follow through with your strike in the same path you wish the chip to be removed.

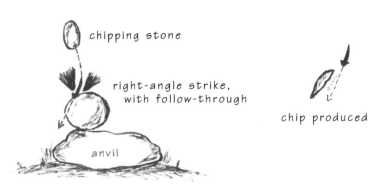

chipping stone

right-angle strike, with follow-through

chip produced

anvil

4. Once you have your chip, you can then pressure chip to form your arrow point. To accurately replicate the ancestral way of crafting an arrow point, obtain a bone from a local butcher (or steal one from your dog) and rough-round the bone with a file. Use this pressure chipper to flake away smaller chips from the arrow point until you have formed a triangular, tapered-stem, or leaf shape to your arrow point. You may also pressure chip with a common nail that has been driven securely into the end of a short, rounded piece of wood (so you can chip at the arrow point with the exposed head of the nail).

smaller rock is then rough-shaped with chipping stone

PRESSURE CHIPPERS.

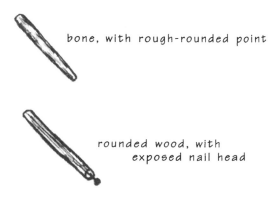

bone, with rough-rounded point

rounded wood, with
exposed nail head

flakes are removed with pressure
chipper to achieve finished shape;

flakes in layers, with careful,
patient chipping on each side,
in the order shown.

If you want to lash your arrow point onto the end of a spear-stick or an arrow, create side notches on each of the longer sides of the arrow point. Work on both sides of the arrow point to create the notch and to prevent your arrow point from fracturing. When the notches are finished, dull any sharp edges to prevent cutting or fraying of the lashing.

While the original purpose of most traditional American crafts was to assist or ensure survival, the crafts also served as a means of communication. That is, each craft gave voice to the culture of the people who created it. The American Indian blanket provides a provocative example of such a melding of survival need and cultural voice. While the primary role of the blanket was to keep warm, the American Indian blanket (first made out of animal skins, and later woven from available wools and hairs on looms and distaffs, or spindles) was also an article of dress that signified status, authority, individual identity, and, surprisingly, mood. A 1900 study of Southern Plains Indians included photographic as well as firsthand evidence of how personal states of being were exhibited by the way an Indian blanket was worn on the body: folded over the arm (to show individuality as well as to symbolize tribal belonging, such as during a dance), casually positioned over the shoulders (to show attentiveness), wrapped snugly around the waist (to reveal tribal authority or to convey a desire to speak to or address others), drawn tightly across the shoulders (to show doubt, anxiety, or hesitation), pulled across the waist and draped over one shoulder (to convey displeasure, to issue admonition, or to express anger), or positioned so it covered the body from head to toe (to show admiration or courtship intentions).

Imbued with more than just practical application to everyday life, the American Indian blanket was thus a poetic statement that was given voice by the wearer and the culture of his or her own tribe. The Cheyenne, for instance, often used the blanket in their courting ritual. "When a young man became fond of a young woman," wrote Father Peter Powell in his two-volume history of the Cheyenne people, *People of the Sacred Mountain,* "he went close to the lodge in which she lived, wrapped in his robe or blanket, so that his head and

BLANKET DESIGNS, WITH TETON DAKOTA NAMES.

≡	trails	⊕	four directions
▂▟▓▙▂	mountain, hill	⏍ ⏍	horse tracks
╪	dragon fly	◆	feather
⧘	lightning	▽	leaf
△	tepee	✴	morning star
⊔⊓⊔	forked tree	◆ ◆ ◆	whirlwind, feather breath of life
M	clouds	⋈	turtle

face were covered. There he stood, waiting for her to come out on some errand. When she passed on her way to get water or gather wood, or on her return, he stepped up beside her and threw his arms and his blanket around her, covering her with his blanket. Holding her fast he began to talk to her, hoping that she would listen to him."

Just as the wearing of the blanket had something significant to communicate, so, too, did the **pattern that was woven into the blanket**. Lines, crosses, and designs were considered to be a narrative of the events in an individual's or a tribe's life: the straight lines or horizontal stripes might tell that the people followed many trails; the crosses might indicate mountains or that the people traveled in all four directions on their journey; the double-cross design might signify the search for water and safety. Other common symbols that were woven into blankets—bolts of lightning, horse tracks, turtles, the morning star, tepees, the four directions, birds, and so on—were inspired more by native experiences than by aesthetics.

The American Indian blanket was a prized possession that accompanied a tribe member throughout his or her life: from infancy, when the child was wrapped in a soft, warm blanket and carried on the mother's back, nestled securely in a fold of the mother's blanket; through adulthood, when blankets were given as gifts to commemorate important milestones and achievements; in maturity, when blankets were used to convey an individual's identity as well as to barter; and in death, when the tribe member was wrapped in a favorite blanket for transition to the next world. Today many Indian people recognize that the traditional Indian blanket, woven in the old ways on handlooms, makes a statement of their sense of belonging not just to the modern Indian community, but also to their ancestral Indian heritage. Well-known and respected Lummi Indian blanket maker Fran James lives on the 12,500-acre Lummi Reservation on a peninsula 100 miles north of Seattle, Washington. Determined that the crafts of her tribe will live on, she bought a loom from the tribe twenty years ago. Both she and her son—who has become skilled in reproducing the twill weave characteristic of Northwest Indian blankets—barter the blankets they make with owners of local flocks for wool so they can make blankets for wholesale and prepaid mail order commission work. "The old blankets were made from mountain goat wool and dog hair, materials unavailable now," explains Fran. "Today we make them the same way but from sheep's wool. Only the materials have changed. We use only natural wools and natural colors; we use no dyes."

Today, even in non-Indian communities, the gift most often given to a newborn boy or girl is a blanket. More often than not, it is one that has been knitted, crocheted, or quilted by an older family member. One of the most treasured family possessions is still the handmade quilt, which is lovingly passed down from generation to generation. Young people and baby boomers fill adult education programs that offer quilting classes so they can learn how to make their own quilts. And, in many locales, the average age of quilting bee members is steadily dropping as young women (and even a few young men) seek to hold on to the time-honored American tradition of making a handmade blanket that will not just warm the body but will also soothe the mind with the stories communicated by each carefully chosen panel.

Countless other traditional American crafts are being created today in the "old ways"—by using materials provided by nature; by following the traditional, or ancestral, methods and tools for construction; and by adding individual craftsmanship and creativity for unique detailing and style, so each completed craft is, as it was in the past, one of a kind. Birchbark canoes, baskets woven out of sea grass or strips of bark, beaded moccasins, brooms, beeswax candles, stoneware and earthenware, totem poles and other wood carvings, cornhusk crafts, tomahawks, straw hats, horsehair ropes, brain-tanned hides, snowshoes, children's sleds and sleighs made entirely from wood, and treenware (or household ware created from trees) are just a few crafts from the past, created from nature's raw materials and instructions passed down from generation to generation, that are being preserved in the present by master craftspeople. These crafted items, as well as countless others, are being replicated today because of an intense appreciation for the "wild wisdom" that once helped America's early settlers survive in a harsh and rugged environment.

Yet such intense appreciation can be expensive; today's traditional American crafts often command high prices. A Fran James blanket, for instance, costs $500, with reduced prices for orders of two or more blankets. A birchbark canoe made in the Malecite—Maine and New Brunswick Indian—style sells for about $400 per linear foot, with the most popular model being the sixteen-footer. Beadwork belts run $250 and up. Pomo Indian Baskets, considered by many experts to be the most beautiful in the world, are small, bowl-shaped baskets woven in coilings of sedgeroot over willow sticks; decorated with feathers, beads, shells, and abalone woven into the construction. These baskets can take years to make and cost from $200 to $2,000. And adult beaded moccasins made with rawhide soles and brain-tanned deer or elk tops can cost from $175 to $300 a pair.

While it may be easy to see what value, in terms of dollars, the creation of traditional American crafts has, you may find it hard to relate today to the *need* to create such crafts, which depend on skills developed and honed from a knowledge of wild wisdom. You might wonder what purpose knowing how or why America's Indians or early settlers lived off the land has in your everyday life; after all, nature is no longer mankind's pharmacy, grocery store, clothing distributor, house-and-hearth catalog, or furniture supplier. Instead, your world is crammed full of manufactured and processed items—from the toothpaste and toothbrush you use in the morning to the alarm clock you set at night. Today it takes a fleet of moving vans to relocate a three-member family; great quantities of items in every style, color, shape, and size are crammed into closets, drawers, cabinets, chests, attics, basements, freezers, and garages. "Think about your breakfast today," suggests *Maynard Beacon* writer Bee Brahm. "You didn't plant, tend, harvest, grind, or shape corn into flakes; you pulled a box out of a cupboard. You don't have to keep or milk a cow, because you have milk in the fridge." Hunting and fishing are now enjoyable hobbies, not tasks necessary for your survival. A fireplace in your home or apartment is a luxury, not a necessity for cooking and staying warm. Candles are used as a prelude to romance, not as the primary source of light. Water comes from a faucet, not a clear mountain stream. The wearing of animal furs sparks protest and outrage. Packages are delivered overnight, great distances covered in hours.

Why, then, labor painstakingly for months over the construction of a birchbark canoe, using only an ax, awl, and crooked knife, when fiberglass canoes in every color, shape, and size can be obtained in less than a minute by making a phone call and having your credit card handy? Why spend the time collecting and then carefully weaving sea grass into a basket when manufactured baskets are cheap and easy to obtain? Why use high-quality, handsplit wood-frame snowshoes to gently and quietly explore the woods after a deep snowfall when the mere turn of a key can power the engine of a snowmobile, allowing you to zip effortlessly across miles of snow?

Very simply, the answer is this: *because you live in a world where things have been created for your enjoyment rather than in a world where creative things can be made by you, to your great enjoyment.* Natural creativity is as much an exciting exploration of America's past as it is a fascinating journey to discover the variety of ways in which you are linked with that past. Natural creativity is as much an experiment with your own imagination as it is an experience you share with the imagination of your ancestors. Natural creativity courses deep within you—in your heart and in your soul—just as it once pulsed through the heart and soul of those who lived long ago. William Beebe, American scientist, explorer, and author, described this intense ancestral connection of present with past as he stood on the high roof of his New York home on a chilly evening in February 1940 and watched the sun sink below the distant Jersey shore. "All around where I now stood there were great primeval forests of oaks and chestnuts, and between the trees fires gleamed here and there, with Indians gathered about," he noted. "Instead of automobile horns, the howls of wolves came from the distance, and in place of the thousands of footsteps upon pavements, there were rustlings in the underbrush and drowsy murmurings of wild turkeys settling to roost."

Step outside your home or apartment at sunset or late in the evening; look up at the sky—truly look—at the cosmic spectacle above you. What you see is what so many others have seen before you. Turn back the hands of time to one, two, or three hundred years ago, and you become part of an Indian village. You fish and hunt and grow maize. You grind and then cook your corn meal; you call it *sup-*

paun. You wear a robe and leggings that you made out of fur and skins. Your feet are nestled in soft, warm moccasins that you have painstakingly and beautifully decorated. You know the secret of making brilliant pigments—red, blue, green, brown, white, yel-low, and black—from the earth and nature's bounty. You have fashioned your own weapons—bows and arrows, war clubs, and **hatchets**—and have used them well to survive. You have made your home out of hickory

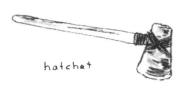

hatchet

saplings, planting them firmly in the ground, bending their tops, and then tying them together. You then split saplings and wove them in and out of the walls, finishing this home by thatching the whole with bark. You and the many members of your family have lived com-fortably and snugly together within this shelter, through all kinds of weather.

Thousands and thousands of sunsets later, evidence of this past village and past lives are gone from the ebb and flow of your every-day life. But the reality of their existence is still vital and vibrant in your world. For America's ancestral heritage and the birth and devel-opment of natural creativity have influenced nearly everything you use today. Take where you now live, for instance. The little-known reality of America's early colonization is that the first homes built by the settlers were not cozy, Abe Lincoln–style log cabins but bark wigwams or dugout caves. Like the country's earliest inhabitants, the settlers made use of what was readily available from nature. The dugout caves, which were prevalent in New York, Massachusetts, and Pennsylvania, were built into embankments, with three sides of earth cased with wood, and a fireplace built at the back. The dirt floor was covered with planks; the fireplace and chimney structure were made of fieldstone and sticks of wood held together by mortar made of clay and grass. In New England, dome-shaped wigwams were popular. Constructed out of small poles stuck in the ground and covered at the top, the shelter had a fireplace at one side and a wood door, rather than a mat, attached with hinges. There was even a win-dow covered with birchbark lining or oiled paper that let a little light into the gloomy room. A layer of straw covered the floor; at night each family member rolled into skins and slept on the straw. An occasional log home was erected, but log cabins were not the usual first shelter of the early settlers.

After the need for immediate shelter was fulfilled, greater ingenuity and creativity were employed by America's early colonists as they used nature's raw materials to make things useful to their survival more beautiful. From one-room houses came two-room homes with a loft or attic. Then two-room homes were built with a central chimney and a lean-to—a room built at the back of the house that was used as a workroom. Then homes were constructed in which the attics were finished off and divided into two bedrooms, with a new attic added on top. Then more chimneys and more rooms were added until the end result was a fine colonial home, many of which are still standing today in New England communities. Where you live today is simply a modern version of the one-room house that grew and grew.

The relationship that America's early settlers forged with nature—a relationship that enabled them to discover and use raw materials in increasingly unique and ultimately more beneficial ways—led to their wild wisdom. Settlers made good use of local natural materials. The thatched roof of homes built near the sea, which was made from ocean grasses or rushes, shed the rain and kept out moisture so well that lots were assigned to each settler for the raising of grasses for reroofing or building new homes. Wood was used predominantly in New England because of the vast forests there; fieldstone and ledge in Pennsylvania and parts of New York; brick in Maryland, Virginia, and the South; red sandstone in New Jersey. A small entryway was added to New England homes because of the icy blasts and gusts of snow that entered the warm house whenever the door was opened. In the warmer South, however, there was no need for small entryways; instead, spacious halls sometimes ran the length of the house.

America's early settlers continued to put their creative and physical energy into making the things they had created for their survival into more beautiful and more functionally beneficial variations. Through experimentation with a variety of other raw materials, they continually honed their wild wisdom. Gradually, however, man-made materials and manufacturing processes led mankind away from an interdependent relationship with nature—taking only what was needed for survival and replenishing depleted supplies to create a flourishing source of sustenance—and toward independence from nature and reliance on industrial growth and technology. Over time, nature became mankind's overworked servant, and everyday life was forever changed—appreciation of nature turned to depletion of nature.

Natural creativity gives you an opportunity to join in spirit with America's early inhabitants: to see nature as they once did, to experience nature with the same reverence and wonder, and to craft things in ways that they, too, might once have crafted. You can develop your own wild wisdom by visiting the many wild places nature offers—woods, countrysides, seashores, lakes, and streams. Natural creativity encourages you to collect interesting treasures while you are out in the wild spaces, then return home to see what you can make out of what you collect. It is an experience that can be both educational as well as enlightening. As Ernest Hemingway once said about creativity: "From things that have happened and from things as they exist and from all things that you know and all those you cannot know, you make something through your invention that is not a representation but a whole new thing truer than anything true and alive, and you make it alive, and if you make it well enough, you give it immorality."

Exercising Your Ancestral Natural Creativity

1. Tour an old New England home open to the public (such as the Alcott House in Concord, Massachusetts, or Hawthorne's "House of Seven Gables" in Salem, Massachusetts) or visit an historic village-style site such as Williamsburg, Virginia; Plymouth Plantation in Plymouth, Massachusetts; or Old Sturbridge Village in Sturbridge, Massachusetts. Note the natural materials used in the construction of the homes as well as some of the naturally creative ways in which the homes are decorated and furnished.

2. Attend a Native American powwow, or celebratory gathering, of one or more tribes. Observe some of the traditional Indian crafts that are on display or for sale. Talk to the craftspeople so you can learn about the importance each craft had to an Indian or a tribe. Listen to the drumming and watch the dancers in their costumes as they perform some of the Indian rituals particular to their tribe.

3. Fences have always been an interesting part of the landscape. The first type of fence was the log stockade, which was built for protection against the Indians. Homesteaders built fences around the house, yard, garden, and tilled fields to keep out cattle, poultry, geese, and swine, which were allowed to roam free. Different sections of the country originated different styles of fencing. In the South, the snake fence—so named because of the way it wound along the ground—was constructed by rails laid zigzag on the ground, with each end lying across the end of the adjoining rail. A second rail was then laid above the first in the same fashion; as many rails were laid as were needed to achieve the desired height of the fence. In the West, the split-rail fence was made by driving into the ground posts in which holes had been made to hold the rails of the fence. In the North, stone walls were more common than wooden rail fences; they were created or added on to during spring, when the fields were plowed and stones would be turned up. Stone walls could be as high as four or five feet; low walls sometimes had a rail-fence addition on top to achieve a desired height. Using readily available natural materials, design and build a fence for a side of your yard or for a small herb or vegetable garden.

4. In early America, paint was made from the clay in the soil, which was then mixed with egg whites, whey, or skim milk. To obtain various colors other than the red, yellow, and gray of the clay, dyes were made from barks, berries, and flowers. In the springtime, a fresh coat of paint was usually added to all the rooms in the home. Some of the more popular colors were Pumpkin Yellow, Turkey Red, and Wagon-Wheel Blue. Collect a variety of small containers of craft paint colors. Then experiment with mixing colors until you come up with the right color combinations to make the correct shades of the three popular colors as well as three more that capture America's colorful past.

5. Some early **clothespins** were whittled by hand. Use a jack-knife to fashion a clothespin from a small piece of wood.

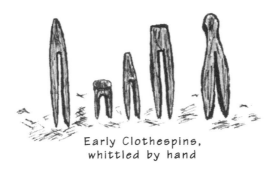

Early Clothespins,
whittled by hand

6. One of the earliest methods of obtaining light was by the use of pine knots from the pitch pine. Both the Indians and the early settlers used these knots indoors and outdoors; the colonists called the wood candlewood. Historic accounts from that period in America's history often mention that a pine knot was placed on the hearth to give light for reading. One night, use only candlelight while preparing dinner, eating, and then reading before going to bed. Devise ways to increase the illumination from a single candle.

7. In New England, one of the most important tasks of spring—and one that was usually quite festive—was sap gathering for making maple syrup and sugar molasses. Nearly every family had a grove of maple trees, and the amount of sap that was obtained was usually enough to provide the family with its own maple sugar and syrup as well as a modest income. When the long process of sugaring was complete, a festive evening was enjoyed. Neighbors gathered and sampled some of the thick sugar molasses on snow, sang, and played games. Plan your own maple sugar potluck dinner party. Ask friends, family members, and neighbors to explore old cookbooks and experiment with a recipe for a main dish or a dessert made with real maple syrup that they can share at your potluck party. Encourage recipe swapping during the gathering.

8. Long ago, besides having a grove of maples, nearly every family living in the country had an apple orchard. Apples were used to make cider, applesauce, apple butter, puddings, and pies. Gather your family or housemates together to make and bake an apple pie.

Purchase your apples from an orchard or farm stand or, better still, pick your own. Divide up the pie-making duties into making the crust and creating the filling. Leftover apples can be eaten raw or baked; made into applesauce; or sliced to make sun-dried apples, which can be placed on a rack and dried on a sunny windowsill.

9. Centuries ago, each family would place its own stamp on the butter they brought to market—a cow, a floral pattern, an acorn, and so on. In effect, the stamp was a brand name, signifying to the purchaser the purity and freshness of the butter that family was known to produce. Create your own stamp out of a block of wood—by whittling a design that can be pressed into a soft surface—or collect something from nature that, when pressed into a soft surface, leaves a distinctive design (use modeling clay to see what your pattern looks like). Whenever you make gifts that display your natural creativity, place this stamp on the object (use a printing ink to display the design) or on a gift card to proudly show that you are the creator.

10. Visit your local library or historic society. Research what life was like for your region's early inhabitants. Find out how those people made a living, then seek out those today who are pursuing similar livelihoods to discover any wild wisdom they may be using today.

2
WILDCRAFT GUIDELINES: *Natural Creativity Consciousness*

The native Americans were astounded at the size of the early European sailing ships. Where, indeed, did trees grow to such a gargantuan size— large enough to hollow a vessel of such proportions?
> —artist, historian, and writer C. KEITH WILBUR, from *Indian Handcrafts*

WHEN THE AMERICAN INDIANS of the Northeast needed water transportation, they built a **dugout canoe**. First, they selected a giant white pine tree. Then, they patiently and diligently burned a portion of the tree and axed away the char, ultimately leveling the tall tree. The top and the branches were removed to give the trunk a desired length. The bark was stripped. Further controlled burning, along with chipping and scraping away the char, continued over several days until the inside of the trunk was hollowed out. Simple paddles were fashioned from wood, and the Indians were then ready to paddle across lakes or up and down rivers and streams.

Algonquian dugout canoe. A.D. 1450

In the Indians' experience, it took only one tree to make a dugout. At their first sighting of a European sailing vessel, the Indians could only ponder the creation of such a vessel in terms of the one gargantuan tree that it must have taken to make it. Learning the total number of trees that had been felled in order to construct that one vessel, which was just one vessel in an entire *fleet* of similarly constructed vessels, was the Indians' first introduction to the nation's future practice of natural-resource wastefulness—a practice that has, over the centuries, devastated, depleted, and destroyed once plentiful natural raw materials.

Once, America was a land of sustainable resources, primarily because mankind took only what was needed. Delicate ecological balances were maintained to promote the life and beauty of the plants, animals, earth, and water. But over the years, slaughter, poaching, pollution, urban development, construction, water diversion, wasteful living, and tons of waste and refuse have played a part in compromising the integrity and fertility of the environments of many wild natural resources. While mankind has recently become much more sensitive to conservation issues, and while much has been and is being done to restore that which has been depleted or impacted, caution still needs to be exercised in exploring your natural creativity.

Thus, the first and most important natural creativity guideline is *practice conservation awareness*. One of the biggest challenges you will face when looking for natural raw materials is what *not* to collect. Nature is so full of interesting objects that you may be tempted to squirrel away everything the moment you see it. Try to be selective, however, for the impact you make on the natural resources in your area needs to be of primary concern. Collect natural treasures in moderation and with care; always keep in mind that nothing in nature is endless, especially if it is wasted or abused.

You still can, as your ancestors have done before you, make beautiful and useful objects from natural materials without depleting the supply of those materials. To do so, collect only from a sustainable resource—one that will continue to exist even after you have taken what you need. Never pick or disturb an endangered species of plant. Never remove a shell from the ocean or beach that contains a living creature. Never promote the death of a living sea creature by pulling it from a rock, taking it out of a tidal pool, or picking it up from the ocean floor. Once you find a good example of a certain shell, let the others be. Never uproot a tree from its location. Never cut tree limbs from a tree just to collect them; obtain healthy limbs from scheduled pruning or from the ground just after a storm. Never transplant flowers, herbs, or weeds from the wild into your own garden; whenever possible, cultivate your own flowers, herbs, and fruits. Never take more than what you need for a particular project; pick up ten pine cones from a forest floor rather than fill ten grocery bags. Share any excess with others, or return the excess to its original site. Never pull a plant out of the ground by its roots; always cut a stem cleanly. Never pick a wild-flower or weed if you see only one or two plants in a large area. If you *must* pick a plant from a group, a good rule of thumb is to take only one plant if at least four other healthy plants remain untouched within in a three-foot radius.

Flat-clawed Hermit Crab. : Cape Cod to Texas

Too, stay out of protected areas such as sand dunes, nesting sites, and natural refuges. Whenever you are so advised, always stay on maintained trails. Refrain from using state or national parks as a source of natural raw materials; the parks are for the learning and enjoyment of everyone. Promote future growth in whatever you collect. For example, if you are gathering seed pods, wait until the seeds are ready to be dispersed before you collect them; shake the seeds free as you collect the pods to continue the plant's life cycle in that area. And remember that some ecosystems are so sensitive and have such a fragile balance that they should be avoided completely.

Bearing all these recommendations in mind, recognize that it is your responsibility to know about endangered plants and protected areas where you live, vacation, or visit. Ignorance disregards the natural world; knowledge preserves, protects, and nurtures all life on earth. Check out conservation bulletins and protection lists, which are available from any local park, community conservation commission, or state or national conservation agency. Familiarize yourself with them, respect the regulations, and encourage others to do so.

Become more willing to explore some of those locations you might not normally think would have interesting and plentiful natural raw materials, such as alongside waste areas and dumps; at the edges of parking lots, shopping malls, and in drainage ditches; and in private lands such as farm pastures (but only after you obtain the owner's permission to forage and collect).

❧

Before you set off on your natural creativity collecting expeditions, keep in mind the second natural creativity guideline: *safety first*. Whenever you journey into the woods, along streams, or across pastures and thickets, dress according to the task rather than the weather, and with a higher regard for your safety than for your comfort. In other words, even in warm weather wear thick-soled shoes or hiking boots, heavy socks, and rugged clothing that will protect your arms and legs from scratches, bites, and burns. Wear tapered-leg slacks or sweatpants with elastic at the ankles, or tie pant legs at the bottom, to safeguard against ticks. Carry gloves suitable for working outdoors (some garden gloves may be too thin to protect against prickers). Use insect repellent and sunscreen in the summer; dress in layers in the winter. Wear a hat. Familiarize yourself with plants such as poison ivy, poison oak, poison sumac, and **stinging nettle**—and then stay away from them! Be aware of which insects, reptiles, and arachnids you might encounter in a specific area. If you wish to collect a stick, rock, or weed, gently tug at it *before* you pick it up to make sure you are not disturbing a bee's nest or arousing a slumbering snake or scorpion.

Stinging Nettle.

Use common sense at all times. Refrain from stopping your vehicle on the side of a major highway or near a busy intersection. Never attempt to cross a freeway or other busy thoroughfare. Bridges are not safe locations to park a vehicle, neither is the side of a narrow road or a soft shoulder off the road. Park only in designated or safe areas; travel by foot, cross-country ski, snowshoe, canoe, or mountain bike to locales where parking a vehicle would present a hazard to yourself or to others. While on foot, never venture out onto ice—no matter how thick you think it is or how shallow the water is beneath the surface—and be particularly careful when walking near the edges of marshes and ponds. Sometimes the mud is so deep and so thick that it can act like quicksand, preventing you from extricating yourself without a lengthy struggle or even assistance. Pay particular attention to how you dress during hunting season; don a bright orange vest, gloves, and hat, but keep in mind that such clothing is not bulletproof. Since some trigger-happy hunters react to what they hear rather than what they see, it might be a good idea to stay out of the woods until hunting season is over.

Because travels out into the wild can sometimes be treacherous and more demanding than you think, you may wish to include another or others on your collecting trips. This is wise not just from a safety standpoint for women (to present a "strength in numbers" deterrent to assault) but also to ensure help in case of injury. Foot blisters, heat exhaustion, or a twisted ankle can sometimes place your life in danger; the buddy system provides vital help in the event of unforeseen emergencies. Safety aside, there are added benefits of collecting with others: the company and comradery of like-minded individuals as well as the enthusiasm and creative energy generated from learning how your friends creatively gather and process their own natural raw materials.

Safety first also includes making sure you carry enough water on both hot and cold days to stay well hydrated; figure at least a cup of water for every hour of foraging in the winter and for every half hour in warm weather. Even if you feel parched, never drink from a river, stream, or lake—no matter how clean it appears or how much wildlife (fish, waterfowl, deer, moose, and so on) it seems to support. Animals can tolerate contaminated water far better than humans, so it's just not worth the risk of poisoning or parasitic infestation.

Take along high-energy snacks such as dried fruits, nuts, athlete's endurance bars, granola, and peanut butter on crackers; they will be welcome treats when your collecting takes longer than you had anticipated or when you want to take a rejuvenating break. If you find yourself hungry and without food, do not taste any plant, fruit, or mushroom in the wild unless you can *absolutely, positively* identify it as a wild edible safe for human consumption. Even when you can identify a wild edible, avoid ingestion unless you are certain that it is the proper season for harvesting the plant (for example, wild asparagus is delicious young but toxic at maturity) and that eating the plant or fruit raw is safe (for example, marsh marigold leaves are poisonous raw but edible when sufficiently cooked).

Finally, collect only what you can easily carry out. It is much easier to make several trips carrying light loads than it is to heal a strained back or pulled muscle.

With conservation awareness and safety first in mind, the third guideline for exercising your natural creativity is *carry the right tools and supplies* for collecting. Be prepared not just for those things you are planning to collect—such as shells at the seashore—but also for other natural materials you may come across that you might like to collect—such as driftwood, dried seaweed, and sea glass. Here is a short list of some of nature's raw materials that you might find on your forays to a variety of outdoor locations:

- abandoned birds' nests
- abandoned spiders' webs
- acorns and other nuts
- animal bones, skulls, and teeth
- animal tracks (from which clay/plaster of paris impressions can be made)
- antlers
- artifacts such as arrow points, pieces of pottery, etc.
- bark
- berries and other fruits
- cave and rock art (not for collecting, but for making rubbings or sketches)
- clay
- corn, corn husks, corn stalks, corn silk
- dead butterflies, moths, and other interesting dead insects
- dead wood and driftwood
- dried seaweed and other dead sea life
- egg shells
- feathers

- fern fronds
- flowers and flower petals
- fossils
- gourds
- leaves
- lichens
- logs
- minerals and gemstones
- mosses and mushrooms
- palm fronds
- pebbles, rocks, and stones
- pinecones and pine needles
- pods and seeds
- sand
- sea glass (considered a natural material because of the ocean's effect on the glass)
- shed snake skins
- shells
- tufts of animal fur and hairs
- twigs, branches, and sticks in interesting shapes (found on the ground)
- vines
- weeds and reeds

For sojourns into the woods and thickets, canvas or cloth tote bags, knapsacks, or backpacks are a must for carrying acorns, pinecones, leaves, and other ground treasures. A small handsaw is essential for cutting large branches into manageable sizes and for trimming jagged edges on pieces of wood. Pruning shears can be used to cut smaller branches, while a sharp pair of scissors or shears is recommended for cleanly cutting off leaves or flowers so the stems of plants are not torn and the roots remain undisturbed.

One of the more invaluable collecting tools is a sharp pocket knife. A knife is useful for scouring fields and meadows for wildflowers and weeds, for stripping foliage and thorns, and for digging in the ground. A steel pocket knife, or **jackknife**, is all you need, but make sure you have a good one. A good knife usually has brass side plates, strong rivets (to prevent the blade from becoming wobbly after use), and stiff springs (to keep the blade from closing while cutting). The handle should be smooth, from three to three and a half inches in length. A three-blade knife is an ideal choice; you can use the large blade for heavy or rough cutting on your wood-collecting trips and the small blades for close work, such as whittling.

Newspaper or waxed paper is ideal for wrapping and protecting delicate dried materials such as milkweed pods, while a bucket of water is invaluable for preserving flowers that wilt quite soon after picking, such as Queen Anne's lace. A bucket or small pail is also helpful in seaside collecting, as are plastic storage bags. You may wish to use scissors rather than your pocket knife when collecting plants

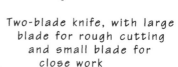

Two-blade knife, with large blade for rough cutting and small blade for close work

and weeds, but remember, safety first. Protect yourself from the pointed blades in the event you stumble by placing any cutting tool you carry with you—scissors, shears, saw, or pocket knife—in a carrying case or safe container when not in use.

Get into the habit of carrying a field guide with you on your collecting trips, not just to help you identify what you are collecting— or what you should not be collecting—but also to press plants or store leaves and feathers in while in the field. You may like to bring along a notebook or nature journal to record sources of raw materials. You can also write down your thoughts in your journal or make rough sketches, which are also expressions of your natural creativity!

❧

Long before supermarkets, butcher shops, and speciality foods stores existed, those about to prepare a family meal of rabbit stew could open their recipe books to find the instruction, "First, snare a rabbit." Centuries ago, your ancestors could only make something out of what they were able to snare, tree, shoot, uproot, catch, unearth, cut down, pluck, gather, sift, harvest, grind, whittle, or collect. Rabbit stew called for not just a rabbit but also potatoes, carrots, and water; a knife to skin the rabbit and cut

Cottontail tracks

the meat into chunks; herbs for seasoning; a source of heat; a spoon to stir and serve the stew; and, of course, a pot to cook it in. Long ago, all these things came from or were created from nature. Thus, natural creativity in the truest sense is about making use not of what you can purchase, but of what you can find.

To replicate this true natural creativity in the modern-day world, where canned stews and electric can openers exist, the fourth natural creativity guideline advises us to *use as many natural raw materials and as few man-made materials as possible* in the creation of any project. Too many "nature crafts" books today call for a multitude of man-made tools and supplies in the creation of so-called nature crafts—such "necessary" tools and supplies as floral picks, floral pins, floral tape, glue guns, foam bases, wire hangers, floral wire, glitter, plastic figurines, artificial flowers and foliage, manufactured decorations, screwdrivers, power saws, sanders, decorative sprays, hand drills, artificial snow spray, plastic eyes, ribbon, styrofoam cones, and so on. Lest you think that using as many natural materials as possible in your creative crafting will be next to impossible, reflect upon the words of American traveler and artist George Catlin, who resided with North American Indians for over a decade and wrote in his journal: "The bark canoe of the Chippeways is, perhaps, the most beautiful and light model of all the water crafts that ever were invented. They are generally made complete with the rind of one birch tree, and so ingeniously shaped and sewed together, with roots of the tamarack, which they call *wat-tap,* that they are water-tight, and ride upon the water, as light as a cork." The Indians also used sharpened and pointed moose bones for sewing the bark, spruce resin as pitch, and spruce fibers to keep the framework and parts together.

To remain true to ancestral wild wisdom, challenge your natural creativity by replacing store-bought items with natural raw material substitutes in your projects. For example, use sticks and twigs to create mobiles rather than wire strands and fishing lines; substitute cordage made from natural materials such as vines and weeds for rope and string; use wadded strips of birch bark in place of cotton; dab on pine pitch in place of glue; and so on.

In addition, keep your workbench tools to a bare minimum: a knife, a hammer, an ax, a pair of scissors, a sharpening stone, a pair of tweezers, toothpicks, paint brushes (which can also be made out of pine needles or the shredded fibers of a stick; see Chapter 3), paints (which can also be made out of earth dyes and crushed berries; see Chapters 4 and 8), common nails, wood-chiseling and whittling tools, a vise, and so on. Refrain from using battery-operated and electric tools.

Try to be independent of man-made and store-bought items, which are often used in crafts projects in order to make the finished objects look "pretty." The point of natural creativity is to use nature's raw materials to craft simple, functional, and attractive objects; each of your crafts will thus have its own beauty from the way you creatively utilize the natural raw materials and uniquely assemble them. There are, however, some exceptions to the use of man-made or store-bought items in natural creativity crafting. These include: baskets, clay pots, prepackaged earth clay (sold in craft stores), manufactured feathers (because real feathers are not always easy to find), beads created from bone or clay, and gemstones and minerals. Too, any items that you might throw out or recycle can be used in your crafting in order to give such items a functional second life; these items include tin or aluminum food cans (which can be used for displaying wild flowers), plastic containers and lids (for mixing and storing dyes), glass jars (for displaying sea glass and other items), wire coat hangers (for making mobiles and for drying herbs and weeds), egg cartons (for storing nuts, pods, and other small collectibles), leftover material from sewing projects, and a light application of an acrylic spray or work fixative to preserve—but not gloss—a finished product.

❧

Natural creativity can be a catalyst for profound explorations of personal discovery as well as a motivator for creative experimentation on your part—for trying out different ways of doing things. A fifth guideline for expressing your natural creativity is *think new thoughts and do old things in new ways.* Imagine, for example, that you want to make a basket from cattail leaves, giant bulrushes, or spruce roots. The fact that American Indians fashioned such baskets—and fashioned them well—does not make it any less of a creative effort on your part. Whatever the end result, no one else has fashioned a basket just as you have, for your materials are different and your style of weaving is uniquely your own. Because of this, you do an old thing in a new way—*your own way*.

As well, you can think new thoughts by making a basket using natural materials that no one else has used before or by combining the new materials with decorative embellishments. The finished product may be pretty, useful, amusing, experimental, or just for fun; however, the most important outcome is not the object that is made or the way in which it was made, but the enjoyment of finding out about the materials and how to creatively employ those materials. One tentative experiment in recreating an ancestral artifact, in making a familiar object, or in devising your own craft can lead to another, bolder trial; greater variations can lead to never ending, ever widening circles of new, creative experiences.

❧

Even though this book emphasizes what to do with what you find on your sojourns out in nature, it is only natural that you may feel an increasing sense of curiosity about what you see and what you gather on your collecting trips. *Be willing to learn something about what you see or collect* is the sixth guideline for exercising your natural creativity. For example, turning pinecones into bird feeders, floral bases, or animal figures is just one part of the creative project. "If it is combined with the fun of finding, collecting, and identifying these cones," writes Virginia W. Musselman in *Learning about Nature through Crafts*, "with seeing the blue sky through the pine tree, watching a squirrel on a branch, walking on the springy pine needles under the tree, smelling them, identifying the tree by the number of needles in each little 'bundle'—these are what give the real *meaning* to the craft project."

The more you learn about nature and the raw materials you collect, the greater your appreciation and interest will be. In fact, you may discover that you enjoy finding out more about pinecones— what types of trees produce what types of pinecones, where the trees grow, what time of year the pinecones form and what time of year they fall from the tree, what the seeds look like, what animals like to eat the seeds, how long it takes a closed pinecone to open, and so on—as much as you do collecting and crafting with them. All such questions not only expand your knowledge and help to satisfy your curiosity, but also serve as catalysts for pinecone art creations that reflect the pinecone's integral role in a vital, living ecosystem.

❦

Because collecting materials out in nature is essential to the process of expressing your natural creativity, you may find that each time you explore and wander about in nature, you become more familiar not just with the natural world around you—an ecosystem that is teeming with life and death and change—but also with the natural qualities of the earth—the leaves, rocks, shells, dirt, flowers, weeds, roots, and so on. As you grow more comfortable being out in nature and more familiar with nature's raw materials, you may begin to see the vital kinship that you have with the living things that share the world with you—or "all our relations," as the Native Americans say. In recognizing your place on the earth not just as an individual being but also as a member of a species that is participating in the tangled network of living, growing relationships, you may begin to see that natural creativity is, in large part, an expression of that sacred dwelling place within you that so many others have shared with you and with nature throughout the years. Because of this, the seventh natural creativity guideline is *readjust the way you look at the world so that you can see nature with new and different eyes.* This new and, perhaps, different vision you develop of the world through exploration of your natural creativity can help to broaden your perspective about your place in the world as well as soften your rigid concepts about how life ought to be lived.

Natural creativity is not just about collecting natural materials and making something out of those materials. Rather, it is about *noticing* natural materials: how they taste, smell, appear, feel, and sound; the integral place they hold in the world through the special function they provide; and the relationship you have with those materials that unifies modern-day thinking with ancient wisdom. Natural creativity encourages you to expand your oftentimes limited view of the world by showing you that there are no boundaries in nature: mountain top merges with bright sky; ocean merges with seashore; spruce trees reach high to the sky and root deep into the earth, thereby melding earth and sky together; fast-moving water polishes rock until the rock becomes an integral part of the stream. Natural creativity is an exciting journey that provides interesting, fascinating, enriching, profound, life-enhancing, and even life-changing connections to the natural world.

Doug Elliott, who today is a nature writer and illustrator, describes in *Wildwoods Wisdom: Encounters with the Natural World* how one of his youthful sojourns into nature guided him to his career:

> Wherever I went, I looked at the plants. Hardly any of them were familiar. I had no field guides, so I couldn't identify them. All I could do was crush little pieces of the leaves between my fingers and sniff. And such smells there were. A few, like bay leaves and eucalyptus, I could recognize and sometimes I knew the family, but the species were all new, and each was a new sensory experience. There were many kinds of pungent sagebrush, aromatic mints, flowery-smelling composites, sweet-scented umbellifers, and more. Each plant had a unique fragrance that filled my head and tingled the recesses of my brain. It is said that the sense of smell provides a direct link to our unconscious, and I think that having those sensory experiences with totally unfamiliar plants accessed a deep connection. The plant world was speaking to me. I knew that I wanted to become more involved with plants in some way.

The sensory experiences that foraging in nature can arouse can also stimulate past memories—childhood reminiscences of times when you once had a strong, close, intimate relationship with nature. For example, the wind that whispers through the pine trees as you walk in the woods may trigger a memory of camping outdoors with your family when you were young. The sound of crickets chirruping outside your suburban apartment window on a hot summer night may remind you of the hot summer nights when you excitedly collected fireflies in a glass jar. The sight of rolling hills covered with snow may spark the remembered thrill of crazily speeding and spinning down a hill on your "flying saucer." The lively music of the spring peeper chorale may urge you to roll up your pants legs and wade into a pond to search for polliwogs.

Those who participate in nature crafting as adults do not, as a rule, undertake such activities because they are educational or even good for them. Such people just naturally like to do things that are fun—and natural creativity can be a lot fun! So, the eighth—and final—natural creativity guideline is to *be a kid again and have fun with nature*. By doing this, you may find that some of the simplest nature crafts—and the ones that bring you the greatest amount of pleasure—are those that are based on things you liked to do as a kid, such as carving wood, picking flowers, or collecting seashells.

With these eight guidelines in mind, get set to embark on a journey of creative exploration and experimentation as you travel to a variety of exciting, interesting, and beautiful natural spaces!

Exercising Your Natural Creativity Consciousness

1. Get a good field guide—one that lists trees, shrubs, plants, and weeds. Study the guide at home as well as take it with you on your collection outings. Remember, it is as important to be able to identify what you are collecting as it is to make something unique out of what you collect.

2. Find out what plants are protected in your area. Then, if possible, try to locate a few of them out in the wild. See what they look like in their natural element. Look closely to discover some of the qualities that make them one-of-a-kind natural treasures.

3. Create a checklist of tools, supplies, and equipment you consider necessary to carry with you on your natural creativity collecting hikes. You may also wish to include other, nonessential, items such as binoculars, a camera, a sketch pad, a magnifying glass, hat netting (to keep mosquitos away), and a first-aid kit. Refer to this checklist whenever you prepare for a collecting trip out in nature.

4. If you are planning a collecting hike in an unfamiliar area, obtain a trail map first or talk with others who know that area. Your collecting experience will be much more rewarding and far more pleasant when you know where you are at all times. Listen to local weather broadcasts before you go outdoors. Be aware of any high-wind warnings or forecasts of heavy rain, thunder and lightening, hail, or heavy snowfall. Time your collecting trip so it ends well before the onset of potentially threatening weather. Dress according

to current weather conditions as well as changing weather conditions.

5. When you go out into nature, walk slowly and take in as much as you can. Give yourself time to investigate everything—from the undersides of leaves to the living creatures in a tidal pool—rather than collect things as fast as you can. Look and listen for signs of wildlife; try to identify birds from their calls and animals from their tracks. All these things will give you information about the area that can alert you to interesting natural raw materials you might not have thought you would find. For example, if you come across animal tracks and follow them, you may find a hidden pond, or if you hear the hoot of an owl in a grove of trees, you may be able to find a discarded feather on the forest floor beneath those trees.

6. If something you collect in nature prompts you to ask a question about it—for example, if you wonder what kind of creature once lived in the sand dollar you found on the beach—go to your local library and try to find the answer. Expanding your knowledge base can stimulate your creative juices!

7. Seek out old Colonial America and Native American cookbooks. Browse through some of the recipes to discover the ingredients that were used and the preparation methods that were employed. Pay particular attention to the wild game (squirrel, bear, moose, hare, deer, quail, and so on) and wild edibles (such as cattail flour, elder blossoms, sassafras, salsify roots, nettle tops, and so on), which were mainstays of the early settlers' larder.

ANCESTRAL NATURAL CREATIVITY CHALLENGE:

CHIPPEWA BANNOCK

Make a trail food for your foraging trips that was once prepared and eaten by Native Americans on their sojourns into the wild.

2 cups cornmeal
¾ cup water
5 tablespoons fat or oil to season
honey to taste and/or ½ cup fresh berries
¼ cup oil for frying

By hand, blend the cornmeal, water, and fat or oil together. Sweeten the batter with honey and/or fold in fresh berries (cut-up strawberries; whole blueberries, raspberries, or blackberries). Heat the oil in a large skillet or cast iron pan. Drop the batter by tablespoonfuls into the hot oil, then use a spatula to gently flatten into cakes. Cook 5 minutes per side, or until golden. Eat hot or cold.

---

8. Read a book, journal, or diary that details early American life. Think about how different your life is from the life of an early settler. Then consider the things you would and would not miss from your own life if you could go back and live in that time period.

9. Learn what your official state flower, state bird, and state tree are. Can you find them nearby?

10. On your collecting trips, take time to feel more connected to the earth. Sit under the shade of a tall tree on a hot day and daydream or meditate. Lie in the grass in a field or pasture and look up at the sky; let your imagination run wild as you watch the clouds gently morph into different shapes. Take off your shoes and socks and dangle your feet in a chilly stream. Place a shell next to your ear and listen to the sound of the ocean it carries within it. Rub a stone that has been smoothed and polished by rushing water against your cheek. Sit outdoors on a clear, starry night and imagine yourself on an out-of-this-world journey from constellation to constellation.

Chippewa kitchen rack

3

WILD WOODS:
Natural Creativity from Forest and Thicket

Ah Nature! the very look of the woods is heroical and stimulating. This afternoon in a very thick grove where Henry Thoreau showed me the bush of mountain laurel, the first I have seen in Concord, the stems of pine and hemlock and oak almost gleamed like steel upon the excited eye.
—RALPH WALDO EMERSON, November 20, 1840, *Journals*

Mountain laurel, with its spectacular springtime profusion of white-and-rose star-shaped flowers, is today known as the state flower of both Connecticut and Pennsylvania. It is also the glory of an Appalachian spring, when thousands of nature lovers make annual pilgrimmages just to see it in bloom. This close relative of the rhododendron is considered by many to be one of the more popular ornamental landscape plantings in America; it is hardy in poor soil, tolerant of shade, and magnificent not just in spring but in winter as well, with its glossy, dark, evergreen leaves.

In the wild, however, this gnarled shrub, or small tree, is a forest understory species that often forms dense evergreen thickets in acidic sandy or rocky woods. Throughout American history, mountain laurel has proven itself to be a valuable member of both forest and copse and has been highly valued both by nature and mankind. Black-throated blue, worm-eating, and hooded warblers often nest in mountain laurel shrubs. Its seeds are consumed by Northern flickers, Carolina chickadees, and ruffed grouse. White-tailed deer eat the foliage and twigs. Even though deer and birds can safely eat mountain laurel foliage, it is toxic to humans and most livestock (with the exception of goats, for some unknown reason). But mountain laurel's toxicity has not made it any less valuable to mankind. In fact, centuries ago, the Delaware Indians would drink a brewed decoction of as little as two ounces of leaves when they wanted to commit suicide. America's ancestors often experimented with and created effective herbal medicines using mountain laurel foliage. An ointment made of mountain laurel leaves stewed in lard was a well-known and often used country remedy for "the itch" and other skin disorders. A salve that included the juice of the leaves was applied locally to ease rheumatism. And many brave souls sipped a small decoction of the leaves to break fevers, banish jaundice, and stop diarrhea and hemorrhaging. While the hard wood had and still has little commercial value, pioneers did use mountain laurel wood in the creation of many beneficial items, including wooden spoons and other kitchen utensils.

Mountain laurel, like so many of the over five hundred species of trees and woody shrubs found in America's forests and thickets, is useful not just in maintaining the valuable woodlands ecosystem but can be creatively used by mankind in a variety of crafty ways. You can fashion a great number of crafted items from the countless natural raw materials retrieved from the wild woods near you. Any creative adventure in the wild woods, however, depends not just upon your ability to find things but, as well, to see deeper than the surface appearance of things—into their meaningful purpose to all living things.

"The forests of America, however slighted by man, must have been a great delight to God," John Muir declared in his 1901 classic, *Our National Parks*, "for they were the best he ever planted. The whole continent was a garden. . . . And in the fullness of time it was planted in groves, and belts, and broad, exuberant, mantling forests, with the largest, most varied, most fruitful and most beautiful trees in the world. . . ." Today, nearly one third of the United States—737 million acres—is forested. More than half of this forest land is in private hands; timber and paper companies own about 10 percent, while other companies and individuals hold 48 percent. The remaining 42 percent is publicly held by federal agencies (34 percent), state agencies (7 percent), and local governments (one percent).

But what exactly is this treasure, this "God's garden"? The forest is a marvelous, self-sustaining community of interactive plants, animals, soil, water, and air that all function together as a living, breathing system in order to feed itself and recycle its own waste in a constant, dynamic way. Each plant in a forest produces oxygen, an element that provides food for caterpillars, squirrels, songbirds, and countless other species of living, growing things that exist only in the forest (such as centipedes and mushrooms), that live in the forest but forage in other ecosystems (such as raccoons and the red-tailed hawk), and that live seasonally in the forest (such as migrating songbirds). Each plant in the forest also absorbs carbon dioxide, thus purifying the air. The trees enrich the soil—which is the organic food of the forest plants—by dropping leaves each fall or shedding dead needles. Without this annual dropping of leaves—along with a large assortment of dead twigs and branches—the soil would lose its nutrient supply and the plants would die out.

When an old tree dies, it decomposes, a process that gradually recycles its nutrients into food for new trees to grow. As this decomposition takes place, the tree is still capable of providing for other living things; for instance, its hollow core shelters animals such as skunks, chipmunks, and woodpeckers. The decaying tree also attracts decomposers such as fungi, ants, bacteria, beetles, mushrooms, and worms, which all work to break down the wood and convert it into soil. The enriched soil is then ready to start a new cycle of growth when a seed is buried by a squirrel, dropped on the ground by a bird, or blown in by the wind.

This natural wild woods cycle of growth and death provides valuable raw materials for exploring and exercising your natural creativity. Those things that trees naturally shed, drop, or lose during wet-and-wild weather—the trees' trimmings, so to speak—are the very things you want to look for and collect. Such trimmings vary widely, depending on the section of the country you live in, but a basic list includes:

- bark
- branches, boughs, and twigs
- fruits/nuts
- leaves and fronds
- cones and pods

BARK

Known as the skin of a tree, bark—especially white birch bark—has always been a valuable raw material in the creation of useful items. From prehistoric times until only a hundred years ago, most northern North America shelters used the outer bark of the white birch tree as a roofing material because of its waterproof, bug-proof, and decay-proof qualities. Northern New England Indian tribes used white birch bark to make baskets, dishes, bowls, arrow quivers, and spoons. The light, waterproof bark was used to make scrolls for ritual ceremonies and as fire-starting tinder, reliable in even the wettest weather. Both Indians and frontiersmen dried and then ground the inner bark into flour for making bread; the bark was also cut into thin strips and then boiled like noodles in stews. The Ojibwas, who were known as "the birchbark Indians" because of the many uses they made of the material, became quite proficient in porcupine quilling, an art form that involves stitching porcupine quills in a decorative design on a finished birchbark box.

Reportedly, containers made of white birch bark were also used for cooking food *over fires* by Alaskan natives; as long as the strong containers were kept full of food, they were apparently fireproof. Similarly strong, long-lasting white birch bark containers, called *mukuks* (meaning pail or container), were used by Alaskans for gathering sap from the maple trees in spring and also for collecting sap from white, black, and yellow birches, which typically yield smaller amounts of sap. This sap, boiled down, produces a tasty syrup not as sweet as sugar maple syrup. The birchbark sap-gathering containers—which averaged seven to ten inches wide, twenty inches long, and about eight inches deep—were made from the tree's outer bark, harvested during the winter or early spring when the outer layer retains a thin layer of inner bark that makes it light and flexible. After the piece of bark was folded to size, it was stitched together with natural cordage, such as that from a spruce root, by using a diagonal stitch, double stitch, running stitch, parallel stitch, or cross stitch. The rim of the container was also strengthened by a whip stitch. Finally, a design was sometimes scratched on the outer layer to denote ownership or for decoration.

But perhaps the best-known use of **white birch bark** in North America was for water transportation. Native American birchbark canoes were made of large pieces of birchbark that were stitched together with the roots of black spruce, Eastern tamarack, or jack pine, and then stretched over and around a frame of white cedar. The stitched seams were then sealed with spruce or balsam pitch. The finished canoe—a true forest creation because it only used tree products — was lightweight, durable, and waterproof. Tribes often established shady, level areas as "boatyards" for constructing their canoes; French voyageurs also picked up the craft and used birchbark canoes to travel throughout northeastern North America.

Native American men collected birchbark in the spring and into June, when the sap was up and when the slit bark practically peeled itself from the tree. Two encircling cuts were first made on either the rooted or cut birch tree—one at the base and the second at a height that determined the length of the bark piece desired (bark wigwams, for instance, often used six- to seven-foot lengths of bark). A perpendicular cut was then made from the first to the second cuts. While finger pressure was often enough to ease the bark strips free, the Algonquian Indians also used stone and wooden spuds, or wedge-shaped tools, to harvest larger strips of bark. When knots and branch scars anchored the bark in an area, a few blows with a stick was often enough to loosen the knot's hold. Such scars were rarely cut off. Oftentimes knots added to the design and attractiveness of the finished product, and so were featured rather than hidden; too, knots were considered by many tribes to be spiritually symbolic. The Chippewas, for example, regarded the white birch tree as sacred, associated with the teacher-diety-trickster Winabojo, who blessed the tree for the benefit of humanity. So the knots and old branch scars on the tree, which appear in the form of upside-down black Vs, were thought to be Winabojo's "thunderbirds."

Once harvested, the fresh bark was worked on as soon as possible. Curling pieces were flattened with weights such as stones; flattened bark or bark that was not fresh could be reconditioned by moistening (not soaking) it with water, making it pliable for cutting, bending, or lacing.

While other tree barks were used in covering wigwam frames—basswood, walnut, elm, ash, chestnut, fir, cedar, and spruce—and for making other bark-related items, white birch bark has been and still is the most attractive and easy-to-work-with bark. Bark crafting today, however, must always uphold forest conservation and preservation. Never deface or cut down a living tree just to collect bark to reproduce an Indian handicraft or create one of your own. Removing even small pieces of the protective skin from a living tree may not kill the tree outright, but can doom the tree to a slow death because the damaged area cannot keep out bacteria, wood-eating insects, or fungi. Collect bark from tree limbs and trees that have been knocked down during a storm; be sure to get to the wood as soon as possible to prevent decay or to avoid further decay if the tree is already weakened by disease. Seek permission from landowners if the downed tree or tree limbs are on private property. Timber that is scheduled (by marking) to be felled for lumber, trail maintenance, or clearing can also be a good source of bark; check with local foresters, tree-farm growers, loggers, or appropriate authorities to obtain permission to harvest the bark from the trees either before or after they have been cut down.

One thing to keep in mind when working with white birch bark, more so than any other bark, is that because white birch bark is so thin and flexible, when peeling a tree the natural tendency of the bark is to curl *exactly opposite* to the way it is on the tree. What this means is that the outer, whiter layer will face the *inside* of any container craft you are making; the darker layer will be seen on the outside. Remember this when you plan your craft; Indian birchbark canoes were always white on the *inside* and brown on the outside.

You can use white birch bark and a variety of other thin-layer barks (not scaly barks, which are too thick and crumbly) to explore a number of natural creativity projects on your own. You can make containers in all shapes and sizes and for all functions—bowls, trays, dishes, boxes, and so on; lace the folded ends together with twine or a strong natural vine cordage and then decorate with dried flowers or designs. You can construct **cylindrical containers** to serve as arrow quivers, pen and pencil holders, pouches, drink and/or soup ladles (fold the bark to create a funnel, lace it together, and then lace

Birch bark
dipper

the funnel onto a whittled stick handle), and decorative and functional baskets (made from woven strips of bark). You can flatten pieces of bark and then use the thin, dry, flattened pieces as paper for sketching or nature journaling or for framing favorite outdoor drawings or photographs. You can dry and then store the bark of white birch or, preferably, black birch in sealed jars; add a teaspoon of the bark to a cup of boiling water, then steep for five minutes to make a spicy cup of birch tea. (To discover this natural flavor for yourself, cut a small twig from a black birch tree and nibble on it; both the odor and flavor of wintergreen will remind you of sassafras soda or carbonated birch beer, a root beer–like beverage still popular in some areas of the country.)

Bark creativity can also include making your own natural lacings for sewing or binding. Cut ¼-inch strips from the discarded branches of black willow, basswood, slippery elm, white oak, hickory, white cedar, or red cedar trees. Use the lacings when they are fresh, or moisten the strips before using if they are dried out.

You can also take the following Natural Creativity Challenge and make your own enchanting backyard birchbark torch lighting for nighttime cookouts and gatherings.

WILD WOODS NATURAL CREATIVITY CHALLENGE:

BIRCHBARK INDIAN TORCHES

Indian ceremonies were often enhanced by the light from these birchbark torches. These torches were also used with night activities such as fishing or hunting.

Make each torch with

- a birchbark strip measuring six inches wide and thirty-six inches long, taken from a dead birch tree;
- a long, sturdy, straight green ("live") stick (taken from the forest floor or a drop branch); and
- a saw or sharp knife.

Fold the strip of bark until it is doubled twice. Make a cut lengthwise in one end of the stick, no more than six inches deep. Slide the folded bark into the slit on the end of the stick so the same amount of bark shows on each side of the stick. Insert the stick firmly into the ground. Light the bark. Extra bark strips can be prepared to replace those that burn out. Too, many torches can be made to illuminate a camping area or backyard patio.

Birch bark torch

BRANCHES, BOUGHS, AND TWIGS

The fallen limbs of trees—all sizes and shapes of branches, boughs, and twigs—can be considered the lumber of the naturally creative builder. One such naturally creative builder—furniture maker Frank Hamm of Weston, Massachusetts—makes a living from his "twig furniture" creations, which replicate the rustic, camp-style furniture invented over a hundred years ago in the Adirondacks. Hamm spends a lot of his time at his town's brush dump armed with a saw, jackknife, and gardener's clippers. He never cuts down a tree—"The wood is beautiful in a tree," he explains—and goes out often after winter storms to find and collect immense amounts of wood. He likes to leave the wood he finds in much the same form as it was when he found it, although he might take along a measuring tape to cut a fairly uniform batch of chair rungs. He prizes any branching shapes he finds; some of his favorite pieces become headboards and footboards for beds that are set with a row of branch pieces that resemble a small segment of the forest. Other odd pieces he finds might end up as whimsically mismatched legs or arms for tables or chairs. Bent branches also become coat hangers; hollow logs become liquor cabinets.

Despite their sometimes strange design, Hamm's pieces are fully functional and worth a great deal of money. Clients pay such prices as $24 for a custom coat hanger, $2,000 for a bedframe, or $4,500 for a hollow-log bar. But, to Hamm, the money is not the only benefit of his craft. He has received an incredible forest education; he is so familiar with the wood now that he can tell the type of tree from its bark. He takes pride in the no-two-are-alike uniqueness of his furniture and, because of this, enjoys experimenting with a variety of different presentations. Most important, he enjoys his natural creativity craft immensely. "Playfulness is really the fun of it," he says. "I try to stay away from preconceptions. I mean for my furniture to last as long as any other good furniture. For me, it's a high art."

But not everything that can be crafted from branches, boughs, or twigs has to become high art. A branch with an interesting shape can be placed, as is, against a blank wall in your home and then adorned with a found bird's nest, acorns, pinecone ornaments, or other imaginative forest finds. A log or branch can be sliced into thin coasters of wood, each of which can be used as a canvas on which to paint, charcoal sketch, or wood burn a forest scene (apply a thin coat of shellac or varnish to preserve your art). A long, straight, sturdy tapered stick with a curve at one end can be made into a walking stick. A small stick or twig can hold up mobiles of feathers or support hangings of pods, cones, and so on. Small branches with interesting twisted shapes can make excellent frames for weaving displays; wind strands of bright yarns in and around the branches in a spiderweb kind of pattern, then display them in front of a window or blank wall.

Larger branches that have **burls** on them—healing welts, or tightly compacted circles of growth that are formed when a tree has been wounded or attacked by a disease—are true wild woods finds. Centuries ago, wilderness travelers and dwellers used to saw the burls off branches, whittle out the inner core, and then use the burl for a drinking cup or bowl. When you find a burl on a dropped branch or log, saw off the burl and then, with sandpaper, slowly and carefully discover the interesting layers and patterns of healing growth that have occurred within the burl. After sanding the burl to a surface you like the most, apply oil or varnish to create a beautiful burl container.

You may also wish to do some wood carving or whittling on your burl or, for that matter, or any of the wood you collect. The simplest and easiest kind of whittling—and a good project to start with to help you get the feel of the knife and what it and you can do together—is bark whittling. Any kind of wood with a smooth bark will do; the thinner and darker the bark, the better. Bark whittling involves thinking about a design ahead of time, then recreating that design in the bark by cutting away portions of the bark: the light portions of the design are the bark pieces you cut away; the dark portions of the design are what remains. While bark whittling sounds pretty easy, it will give you a good indication of how quickly your hands can tire or become sore. Although you may be tempted to wear gloves while whittling, even the most snug-fitting glove will limit your movement and numb the feel of the correct amount of knife pressure you need to use on the wood.

Instead, when you first start whittling, work with softwoods such as pines (select pieces that are free of knots and pitch), cedar, fir, linden (also called basswood), butternut, hemlock, redwood, poplar, cottonwood, willow, or box elder; they will be easier on your hands. Softwoods usually come from evergreen, or coniferous trees, which have needlelike leaves; most hardwood comes from leaf-shedding, or deciduous trees, including the more common ash, bald cypress, beech, black walnut, cherry, hickory, ironwood, maple, myrtlewood, and oak.

When you are ready for more challenging whittling projects, you can try making wooden utensils such as a salad fork and spoon set, a porringer (or wooden cup with a handle), ornamental totem poles, animal carvings, dolls or other figures, or **simple relief carvings** (in which the background is carved out while the figure or scene remains in the foreground). While a good, sharp jackknife is all you really need for simple whittling, you can build up a small knife inventory as you become more interested and proficient in your craft. A skew knife is a more rugged version of a paper-

Buffalo relief carving

trimming knife and can make finer, sharper-looking cuts. A small crooked knife, popular with Eskimos and the west coast Indians, is durable enough to whittle bone, wood, and ivory and, in whittling, takes the place of a woodcarver's gouge. Beyond these few knives, stamina is all you need for hours of working at this ancestral natural creativity pastime.

Sometimes it can be fun just collecting wood drops. When you come across twigs and branches in interesting sizes and shapes, let your imagination run wild. You might be able to see animals in such shapes; with a little creative embellishment, you can create an interesting wild animal display. Or study the construction of Indian shelters and village layouts and, on a large piece of plywood, recreate an Indian village using only found objects from the forest, such as twigs, branches, logs, pieces of bark, and so on. Just-dropped boughs from evergreens that you find in the woods or trimmed boughs from evergreens on your own property—spruce, boxwood, fir, white pine, douglas fir, and cedar—can be used to make seasonal wreaths, hanging ornaments, or a table centerpiece; or they can be placed in a vase of water for a fresh forest display in the home. Adorn large boughs with a variety of wild-bird delicacies—fruits, nuts, seed mixed in peanut butter, and suet—and hang outside a window.

The best time to collect wood is in the winter, after a heavy snow, or after a gusty or rainy day. Take along a saw, knife, clippers, or even an ax to make pieces more manageable for transporting out of the forest. But take care not to destroy naturally interesting shapes of the wood; preserve branching branches, bent branches, and Y-shaped branches. Also, keep your eyes open for decorative wood—dry, weathered wood that has been naturally aged and shaped in interesting ways by a combination of time and the elements. Such decorative wood is so unique that it can suitably be called a finished craft—with no other embellishments—after a light application of oil, shellac, or varnish, if desired.

Before you bring any wood into your house, always check the wood carefully for insects, insect eggs, or decay. If the decay and the infestation can be eliminated by trimming the branch, do so; otherwise, return the wood to the woods or to another outdoor location so it can break down and enrich the soil. Use an old toothbrush or stiff brush to remove any dust or loose dirt from your wood. After the wood has been inspected and cleaned, allow it to dry out before working with it. Store in your basement near a furnace, in a spare room near a heating element, or on an enclosed or protected porch for at least a week; drying time will depend on the size of the piece, the extent of the wetness, and the amount of ventilation and humidity in the drying-out location.

Fruits and Nuts

The majority of trees rely on the wind to carry their seeds away from the parent tree in order to ensure a future generation of trees. But not all trees rely on the wind; some trees use their **fruits and nuts** to entice animals to spread their seeds. Some fruits have a tasty pulp with small seeds that are left behind in an

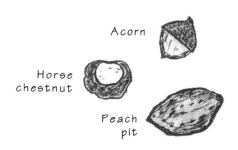

Acorn

Horse chestnut

Peach pit

animal's droppings; wild crab apple trees, for example, rely upon crows and deer to scatter their seeds. Other fruits have a tasty seed, or nut, that is eaten or stored by animals; the stored seeds that are not eaten by the animals, such as the nuts buried by squirrels, later germinate and grow into trees. The one fascinating exception to both types of seed-scattering methods is the coconut-producing palm tree. A mature coconut has enough water inside its shell to keep the young, next-generation tree alive until its roots are well developed; the white flesh provides sufficient food for the young tree. Because the shell is waterproof and the thick, fibrous matting on the shell keeps the coconut afloat for extended periods of time, even if this fruit is captured by a wave and carried out to sea, the thick shell keeps seawater out; if the shell is then tossed from the sea back onto land, it will most likely survive to the next generation.

For this country's early settlers, the fruit and nuts of the fruit-bearing trees were more than just occasional treats; they were a primary source of sustenance and household staples. In the old days, more than eight hundred varieties of wild-woods and home-orchard apples existed in America (even though apples actually originated in Persia; the first seeds and trees reached the Massachusetts Bay Colony only around 1629). Today, many of these unique breeds have long since died out—the lopsided Sheep's Nose apple, the oval Crow's Egg, and the yellow Bellflower; the Horse apple, which was so big and sour that it was considered fit only as feed for horses; and the Limbertwig, which was so named from the distinctive shape and flexible limbs of the parent tree. Nowadays fewer varieties exist; in fact, North Carolina's Agricultural Extension Service claims that 90 percent of the state's commercial apple crop is made up of only three varieties: Red Delicious, Golden Delicious, and Rome Beauty.

Long ago, apples were used in every way possible: to make apple jack, apple brandy, apple wine, apple cider, apple jelly, applesauce, apple butter, apple cake, apple pie, apple crisp, apple pan dowdy, candy apples, baked apples, and dried apples. Great attention was paid not just to the taste of each variety of apple but also to the breed's rate of ripening and its capacity for preservation. Each apple had—as many of today's apples have—a specific season and purpose.

Some were early apples; some were better harvested late. Some were best for slicing and drying. Some were best for making into sauce. Some were best for canning. Some were so juicy they could easily be pressed into cider; some were better suited to long periods of storage.

The most coveted apples were those that were firm-fleshed, which meant that they could be dried. Apple drying was once an important home industry; entire families would peel and slice basket after basket of apples, which were then dried on racks over the cookstove. Sometimes apples were cored and then sliced into rings; the rings were then dried by stringing the slices on a pole. Try drying your own apples today by slicing the apples thinly and spreading them on clean aluminum window screens suspended a few feet above a wood stove or other heat source. The drying usually takes three weeks. You can also sun-dry the slices, but be sure to take them in at night to protect them from the dew.

Apple wood was also prized; the hard, fine-grained wood was used for machinery. The bark was used as a vegetable dye, yielding vivid golds and yellows. Apple games, such as bobbing for apples, were popular children's games, and apple-face dolls were popular childen's toys.

WILD WOODS NATURAL CREATIVITY CHALLENGE:

APPLE-FACE DOLL

Some people believe that the Seneca Indians were the first to make apple-face, or applehead, dolls; they carved them and then used them as "wish dolls." Today applehead dolls are a popular craft in Appalachia. While some craftspeople choose to create elaborately dressed dolls and then paint and varnish the face so the doll becomes a permanent collectible, the more natural method of apple-face doll creation uses no preservative. You may elect to dip your carved apple into lemon juice, dry it, and then lightly shellac it before attaching it to its body. Or you may choose the more natural method of creation, in which case your apple-face doll will just rot away with time.

You can make your own apple-face doll out of

- 1 large apple
- 2 cloves or peppercorns for eyes
- 1 cup lemon juice
- noniodized salt
- a sharp knife
- corn silk, cotton wadding, or other light-colored hair material
- a T-shaped branch, for the doll's body and arms; lace two sticks together in the shape of a cross, with the horizontal stick—the arms—shorter in length than the lengthwise stick—the body
- a long piece of wire
- leftover sewing or rag material

Peel the apple, leaving most of the pulp intact. Gently smooth the surface of the apple with the knife. Use the smoothest side of the apple to make the doll's facial features: the forehead, the nose, the ears, the mouth, the eye holes (insert the cloves or peppercorns at this time), and any other characteristics you desire (a dimple on the chin, for instance, or smile lines at the corners of the mouth). Slide the wire up through the core of the apple and out the top. Dip the apple in lemon juice, then sprinkle it liberally with salt until covered. Bend the wire under the apple to prevent it from sliding off; make a hook at the top of the wire and hang the apple in a well-ventilated area to dry. Do not place near a heat source or in direct sunlight.

Allow the apple face to dry for two to three weeks; the face will wrinkle as it ages, taking on a character all its own. Decorate the head after it has dried, then gently press it onto the stick body (you may wish to make a point at the top of your stick body with a knife for easier insertion). Add hair, and then create and dress the doll in clothes and other accessories.

One of the easiest and most rewarding ways of exploring and expressing your natural creativity with fruits and nuts is through cooking and baking, particularly when you gather your own natural ingredients—pick apples, peaches, or pears at the orchard, for example, or collect your own chestnuts for roasting. But there are also many other ways to be naturally creative with tree fruits.

Using firm fruits, you can make prints in different colors and use them to decorate cards or wrapping paper. Cut apples and pears lengthwise; oranges and grapefruits across the middle; use half shells from walnuts. Dip the fruit in poster or block printing paint, then press lightly on a piece of paper or a sheet of your flattened birchbark.

You can also make decorative dried fruits. One commercial artist discovered his own natural creativity when he peeled a grapefruit one morning—keeping the rind intact—and then absent-mindedly set the peel down on a window sill. Days later, it had dried in such an interesting shape that he began making other "grapefruit sculptures" whenever he had a grapefruit for breakfast. You, too, can explore fruit sculpting with the intact rind of a grapefruit, orange, lemon, tangerine, tangelo, or lime, or any combination of citrus rinds. When your sculpture has achieved a desired form, spray lightly with varnish or shellac.

LEAVES AND FRONDS

When you see a globular mass of leaves and other plant material high in a tree, it is probably the summer nest of a red squirrel. Winter nests are usually built in tree cavities, but are also lined with that most useful part of broadleaf trees, the leaves. All deciduous broadleaf trees located in nontropical zones shed their leaves each fall, sometimes after a brilliant show of color. When the leaves fall, they build up into leaf litter on the forest floor that gradually decomposes. Beetles, worms, toads, toadstools, and many other living things hide or live in the shelter provided by the leaves. Another group of broadleaf trees that are located in the southern, tropical American states—palms—retain their fan-shaped or feather palms, also known as leaves or fronds. Coniferous trees typically retain their leaves, which are often needle-shaped and green all winter long. Thus, each tree in a forest or thicket has its own special "dressing" that can be put to use by the naturally creative wild-woods explorer.

In many Native American tribes, pine needles were used to make excellent basketry that showcased the skills of some of the tribe's best basket makers. To replicate these baskets, however, requires a great deal of instruction, patience, and time. The basic process involves collecting the needles, soaking them until they are supple enough to be tied in knots, then bundling them together to form a coil that is then stitched together with a natural thread such as raffia (which is obtained from a palm tree and is sold commercially; be sure to look for natural, untreated raffia). If you are up to the challenge of pine needle basketry, you may wish to enroll in an introductory course or pick up a book that deals specifically with natural basketry. You can, however, just experiment on your own with the process of soaking the pine needles and then forming coils.

Natural creativity can be expressed simply and beautifully with shed autumn leaves arranged in centerpieces, wreaths, and other clever indoor and/or outdoor displays. Too, a light spray of shellac on a brilliant autumn leaf that has first been pressed can preserve the leaf's color and add stiffness so it can be used in a number of other creative explorations, including Christmas tree ornaments, window hangers, a festive branch door decoration, an autumn mobile, or decorations to dress up the top of a gift box.

Green leaves that are attached to drop branches can be used to make greeting cards, gift tags, and art prints. Just as you did with cut fresh fruit, make leaf prints by dipping or rolling paint onto a leaf cluster and then pressing the painted leaves onto a piece of paper. You can also make a leaf-print identification book from the trees you see. Simply record the type of tree, date, and any other useful or interesting information under each leaf print. Punch holes in each sheet of leaf prints, then use natural cordage to bind the sheets together.

CONES AND PODS

While cones and pods are also known as tree fruit and nuts, their long-lasting qualities and adaptability to a multitude of natural creativity projects has made them one of the most popular subjects of craft books. Because these seed containers provide valuable food for a variety of birds and forest wildlife, collect only spent (empty) cones, which are usually found on the ground under the trees in fall or winter. Some cone-bearing trees retain their spent cones, but if you wait for a high wind, you may be fortunate enough to collect some samples. Lightly brush dirt and dust from collected cones; let wet cones dry out before you work with them. (Some people heat the cones in an oven for a short time at a moderate temperature to kill off any unseen insects.)

Because of the interesting textures and shapes of **pinecones**, a simple display of pinecones in a bowl, basket, or in a bin next to the fireplace can be quite attractive on its own. Pinecones can also be hung in mobiles, placed on the boughs of a Christmas tree, or used as name card holders at the holiday dinner table. If you wish to give cones a gloss, spray with a clear acrylic; cones are quite durable and will last for a long time in any display you create. Use craft books for inspiration in using your pinecones, but try not to be limited to the projects they suggest or the directions given. Use your imagination— combine a variety of pinecones in a project or mix pinecones and other forest-floor finds together to create a true wild-woods craft.

Collect tree and shrub **pods** mainly in the fall and winter. Look for them under acacias, alders, burdocks, castor-oil plants, catalpas, eucalyptuses, locusts, magnolias, maples, sycamores, and others. Dry

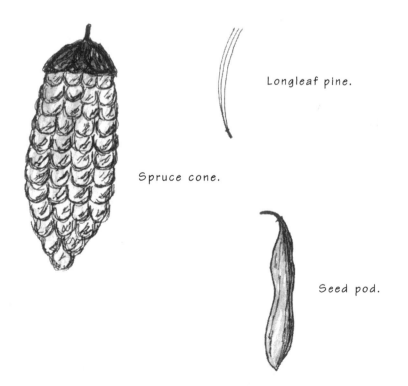

Longleaf pine.

Spruce cone.

Seed pod.

long-stemmed pods by hanging them upside down in a dry, well-ventilated place; individual and short-stemmed pods can be spread out on aluminum screening that allows a free flow of circulation. Store dried pods in boxes with a few mothballs to protect them from insects. You can then make mobiles, wreaths, picture frame accents, pod people, Christmas tree garlands, and a variety of other wildly creative designs!

Exercising Your Natural Creativity in the Wild Woods

1. Even the smallest patch of urban forest can serve as a buffer against the day-to-day stresses of life and can provide you with a rich assortment of natural raw materials to exercise your natural creativity. Explore and collect from as many different urban forests as possible, noting the variety of materials offered in each locale. Keep track of the types of shrubs and trees as well as the assortment of pinecones, nuts and fruits, leaves and fronds, and pods offered. (Obtain a good, pocket-size tree field guide for reference.) Use a notebook and pencils to sketch the shapes of the trees that you see; find out what you can about the wind direction, water supply, and amount of sunlight available in that area by observing the shapes of the trees.

2. Locate a variety of large drop branches or dead trees, then practice stripping bark from them. Let birch bark dry out, then remoisten the bark in order to experiment with its durability and flexibility. Label sample pieces of bark to indicate the types of trees they were collected from, then observe how each changes in appearance over time. Make bark impressions of living trees to capture diverse patterns and textures. To do so, hold a piece of paper flat against the surface of the trunk. Rub lightly with a wax crayon, pencil, or piece of charcoal. Label your rubbing with the date, the tree's name, and its location, then periodically return to the tree to make new rubbings. Note any differences from previous rubbings. Make wall hangings out of your most interesting rubbings.

3. Create rustic candleholders from large pieces of weathered wood. Evenly saw the bottom of the wood so the candleholder will

not wobble or drip candle wax unevenly. Carve out a candle-size hole in the middle of the top of the wood; taper the top if desired; carve interesting patterns into the wood. Then sand and/or varnish the wood. Line the hole with metal or aluminum foil. Insert a candle, then place on a table. Decoratively accent with natural raw materials to create a seasonal or special holiday mood.

4. A long, straight, seasoned 1- to 1 ½-inch diameter piece of wood can be made into a good walking stick for your forays out into nature. First size and then cut the wood to fit you or the person who will be using the walking stick. A comfortable grip on the stick should keep the shoulder even and the elbow slightly above hip level. Use a knife to strip all the bark from the wood. Lightly sand the wood to bring out its highlights. The stick is now ready to use, or you can continue to work on the stick to make an animal tracking walking stick. Use a knife to level-off an area of about five or six inches long at a place on the stick where it will be most comfortable to view a lengthwise display of a few of the more common animal tracks in your area. If desired, use a wood-burning tool or indelible ink to draw the animal tracks. Or level-off a similarly sized area on the stick in which you can keep a record of mountain peaks you scaled, miles hiked, and so on.

5. Tour a maple sugarhouse. Learn how the maple trees are tapped and how sap is converted into syrup. Sample the various grades of syrup. Then make a dessert that uses maple syrup as a main ingredient (not including a topping).

6. Paint with **nature paintbrushes** made from a single branch of an evergreen bough. Simply dab the green-needled end of a branch into the paint. Notice the different designs on your paint surface created by the particular branch. Experiment with different types of coniferous trees—cedar, hemlock, pine, spruce, and so on—for a variety of brush patterns. When the needles dry and turn brown, simply replace your brush with a fresh one!

7. Make a stump doll from a tree branch ten inches long and two inches wide. Peel away the bark two inches from the top of the stump. Paint or carve eyes, nose, and a mouth on this area. Attach hair—use corn silk, strands of grass, or frayed

rope—to the top of the stump. Use extra sewing material or small pieces of rag material to create a head scarf and a neckerchief, or bandanna, for your doll. After you complete your first stump doll, keep your eyes open on your wild-woods forays for pieces of wood that would lend interesting features to another stump doll—knots in the approximate location of ears, smaller branches in the appropriate location for arms, and so on.

8. Explore natural fruit storage offered by the wild woods. In the late fall, gather a large quantity of easily storable fruit, such as apples or pears. Journey into the woods with your fruit. Locate a hollow tree cavity that is low to the ground, such as a hole beneath a fork in the trunk of a large tree. When you find one, clean the dirt and decayed wood out of the hollow. Line the bottom of the hole with dry grass, pine needles, and leaves to create a soft, dry, insulated bed for your fruit. Place some of the fruit on top of the bed, then cover with more dry bedding. Continue layering fruit and bedding until the hole is nearly filled. Pack the remaining space with bedding, then cover the hole with large, flat rocks to keep out water and animals. The following spring, return to the tree to check on your fruit. Some may have turned soft and brown, some may be blemished, but you may be surprised to find that most have stayed crisp and taste delicious.

9. Build a wooden birdhouse from a kit or on your own, from scraps of wood. Mount the house on a piece of wood slightly bigger than the base. Decorate the house with materials gathered from the forest floor and thicket—for example, a short length of branch can be glued to the roof as a chimney; a pinecone tree can be adorned with needles and mosses and adhered near the front door of the house; lichen and mosses can be planted around the front and sides of the house; a whittled totem pole or miniature birchbark canoe can be placed outside the house; and so on.

10. Create a mantle display of pinecone people from forest-floor finds. Use pinecones for the bodies, acorns or nuts for the head, pods for hats, pine needles for hair, and so on.

4

WILD COUNTRYSIDE: *Natural Creativity from Wild Growth*

lerne the hygh and mervlous Vertue of herbes.
Knowe how inestimable a preservative to the helth of man God hath
    provyded
growying every daye at our hande, use the effects
with reverence, and give thanks to the maker celestyall.
                    —English translation of Braunschweig's 16th-century herbal,
                    from *All Good Things Around Us*, by Pamela Michael

THE PEOPLE OF EARLIER GENERATIONS had a profound feeling of respect and reverence for plants in the wild and for cultivating their own plants. While today you may have a backyard, patio, balcony, or window garden because you enjoy gardening as a hobby or pastime; like to beautify your property with flowers or herbs; or feel pride in growing your own vegetables and herbs, the appreciation you feel for growing and using such things nowhere near replicates the appreciation your ancestors felt for the things they found in the wild or cultivated themselves. Your ancestors depended upon wild plants for their sustenance (appropriately, the word *botany*, meaning "plants," comes from the Greek word *boskein*, which means "to feed") and, more importantly, for their survival. Wild fruits, wild flowers, wild grasses, wild roots, wild mushrooms, and wild herbs were all gathered and prepared not just to eat or to use in cooking or

Goose hunting decoy, made of cattail leaves, vines, and grasses

brewing but to cleanse and beautify the body; to prevent and cure injuries, ailments, and sicknesses; to create useful crafts; and to enhance everyday life. Roofs were thatched with reeds and palms. Foods were flavored and preserved with herbs. Spirits and wines were brewed with staple foods—maize (corn), rice, and wheat—as well as fruits and weeds. A variety of ancestral handcrafts, including baskets, **hunting decoys** and snares, children's toys (such as dolls), and musical instruments (such as those created out of gourds filled with dried corn kernels) were designed from dried plants and vegetables. Dyes to color fabrics, clothing, belts, and rugs were created from the juices of flowers, berries, and leaves. Mattresses were stuffed with dried grasses and weeds (which is how yellow bedstraw—*Galium verum*—earned its name). Dried grasses and weeds were also used to raise the surface of woolen cloth when working with it or to comb hair to make it light and fluffy (which is how **teasel**, or Gypsy comb—*Dipsacus sylvestris*—earned its name); and to provide a sense of direction when traveling across the prairie (which is how the compass plant—*Silphium laciniatum*—which grows as tall as nine feet and has enormous lower leaves that always face north and south, earned its name). Decoctions, poultices, teas, and salves of wild botanicals were used as laxatives, diuretics, and emetics; for birth control and during labor; for clearing skin rashes, warts, and burns; and for reducing fevers. In fact, American Indians had such an exceptional knowledge of plant medicinal properties that many of their wild cures

and treatments are used today. For instance, centuries before William Withering discovered digitalis in England in 1785, foxglove

(*Digitalis purpurea*) was already being correctly used by Indians for its cardiac-stimulant properties.

Thus, from the moment humans first began sharing the earth with plants, they established a highly dependent relationship with the greenery. Even if a human being never ate any green, living thing, all of the animals, birds, or fish that person hunted and consumed had been formed from eating plant life. Too, without plant life, mankind itself would not exist, for it was the spread of miniscule green organisms over the hard, cold, barren Planet Earth millions of years ago that eventually prepared the home that would support human life and all other living things.

The tremendous value plant life has to all living things was not lost on your ancestors. Today, you can retrieve some of this old knowledge by learning some of the more common ways plants have been and are still used. Exercise your natural creativity by recreating some of these things today—or expand your creative horizons and discover new ways to work with the natural raw materials in a wild countryside near you!

❧

A few cautionary words before you begin to explore what you can do with plant life in the wild. First, all harvesting of wild edibles—and, most importantly, all sampling of wild edibles—should be done in conjunction with one or more dependable trail or identification guides and/or under the supervision and guidance of someone who is skilled at wild-edible collection and preparation. Better still, many health-food stores, farmstands, and grocery stores offer a variety of wild edibles for consumption, such as fresh herbs, fiddlehead ferns, wild mushrooms, flower petals, and other safe items; try these items rather than forage in the wild on your own or with a guidebook. Even though less than one percent of the known half-million plant species are truly deadly, some plants are toxic to humans or can cause disturbing side effects; it is in your best interest not to take chances.

Remember, too, that while certain natural decoctions, salves, poultices, and other wild-plant preparations have proven to be effective in the treatment of many minor ailments—a ginseng decoction made from the root, for instance, does ease the discomfort of an upset stomach, and fresh aloe juice applied to the skin does help to heal mild sunburns and skin burns—herbal treatments and home-opathies should never be the first, primary, or sole treatment for even the most minor health problem. All health-related problems and their treatments should first be discussed with your physician. Even when you work with a natural healer for your well-being, keep in mind that some herbal remedies can be poisonous or even fatal unless used in moderation. Too, the harvesting of botanicals can be tricky. For example, plant leaves that are gathered after blossoming time may not be as effective as those gathered before blossoming, and some parts of otherwise safe plants may actually be poisonous. For safety's sake, your creation of any wild medicinal or cosmetic treatments ought to start in a health-food store and/or after consulting books and those knowledgeable on the subject.

When you are absolutely certain of the safety of a wild edible, wash it well and then eat it sparingly at first so you can take note of how your body reacts to it. Some wild plants are much higher in vitamins and minerals than normally hybrid vegetables and fruits are, and can therefore be harsher to an individual's digestive system. Too, give yourself a chance to cultivate a taste for an edible's wild-ness. Just as a homegrown or farm-stand tomato tastes different from one purchased in a grocery store, so, too, will wild edibles have their own distinctive flavors, often strikingly different from their hybrid counterparts. Remember, though, that the Colonial Americans had to develop a taste for the famous Indian triad known as "the three sisters"—corn, squash, and beans—which were unknown to them in their native England. Adaptation was the key to their survival; so, too, is adaptation the key to your enjoying wild edibles.

When using fresh herbs to flavor your cooking or to enhance a recipe, keep in mind that fresh herbs have a much stronger flavor than their dried counterparts. Whenever you substitute fresh herbs for dried in a recipe, decrease the amount of wild herbs used so the resulting dish will not be overwhelmed by their flavor.

Wild edibles used for recipes are fairly time-consuming to locate, gather, and prepare; think, for instance, about the time it would take to locate and pick by hand the amount of blueberries you would need to make just one blueberry pie. Too, many wild-plant handcrafts call for the harvesting and drying of the plants *before* you can even start to work with them. What this means is that creating with wild edibles and plants will not be as easy as gathering a grocery bag of pinecones from a forest or going to the grocery store for a quart of blueberries. Natural crafting from the wild countryside requires a great deal of patience as well as a less goal-oriented and more process-centered attitude. As you collect wild plants, take pleasure in walking in the prairies, meadows, fields, and grasslands. Keep your senses open so you can fully appreciate the many details of form, color, and smell that greet you. Then, while your plants are drying, enjoy the fragrances that fill your home.

Finally, be careful of what you pick and how much you pick. Years ago, flowers, herbs, wild berries, reeds, grasses, and weeds grew in real abundance. They could be picked in lavish quantities because there were fewer human beings and more open spaces in which the wild things could grow. Today, however, open spaces are limited, and the number of species available has decreased significantly. Take only those wild things that have a robust foothold in the environment. Know the endangered species that grow in your area. Never collect more than you need. Avoid plants that are growing in or near brackish or polluted water. Be careful, too, of collecting plants growing near highways and next to roads; they may have a buildup of toxic substances from vehicle emissions and road-treatment salts and chemicals. Whenever possible, grow your own herbs, edibles, weeds, and flowers. You will learn much more about the individual plants through the close observation afforded by having them in your own backyard.

❦

Raw natural materials that can be harvested from the wild countryside and used to explore and express your natural creativity are divided into three categories: plants that are best used when they are fresh; plants that are best used after they have been dried; and wild, farm-grown, or home-grown fruits and vegetables, which can be used both fresh and dried. While the botanical names of some plants will sometimes be provided in this chapter (such as Queen Anne's lace, or *Daucus carota*), for the purposes of this book botanical name identification is not as important as what you can create with what you find. Of course you need to determine whether or not a particular plant is endangered or protected, but beyond that, learning

Timothy, a perennial bunch grass also known as "herdgrass" in the New England states

the botanical names of every green living thing in just the small area in which you reside can be overwhelming.

Think of the cattle rancher, for instance, whose grassland plants are his vital tools; beef is, after all, essentially converted **grass**. There are over six thousand different grasses in the world; about seventy-five to a hundred in a given locality. The rancher cannot completely know how to manage his range unless he knows what he is managing, so he must know every grass on his land. But, for you, the naturally creative person, the appreciation you have for living, growing things is much more important; what matters most is what the grasses look like in a weed display, not knowing their botanical names.

The binomial, or two-name, botanical system still in use today was developed by Swedish botanist Carolus Linnaeus in the eighteenth century. In this system, plants are grouped according to their structural likenesses, a grouping that was designed to avoid the confusion created when individual plants came to be known by many common names, depending on where they were found and what the local people originally called them. Queen Anne's lace, for example, is also known as "bird's nest" and "wild carrot." With Linnaeus's naming system, however, *Daucus carota* becomes the two-part name that specifically identifies this plant. The first name is the group, or the genus, to which the plant belongs (*Daucus*). The second name is the descriptive word (*carota*) that, when combined with the first, identifies the given plant as a species.

You will probably find it much easier to learn the common names of each plant you find, harvest, and use because such names describe something about the plant that can help you identify it again out in the wild: its color or scent (skunk cabbage); where it is found (Indian pipe, also known as ghost flower, which is found in dark, gloomy parts of the forest); what familiar object it resembles (butter-and-eggs, also known as toadflax); or what it is used or might be used for (heal-all, also known as carpenter's weed). You might also enjoy exercising your natural creativity by assigning your own descriptive names to the plants you find, just as the original plant-namers did—the Indians, the colonists, the farmers, the hunters, the settlers of the West, and the ancestral healers.

FRESH PLANTS

Flowers and display weeds such as Queen Anne's lace, ferns, goldenrod, and grasses cut out in the wild, gathered at farm stands that allow you to cut your own, or harvested from your own garden or backyard provide you with one of the easiest ways to exercise your natural creativity with fresh plants. Have fun with the colors, sizes, shapes, smells, and textures as you make your own floral arrangements. Be inventive in how you display your fresh flowers. A log or branch can be hollowed out to fit a glass, metal, or plastic container big enough to hold water and display fresh-cut flowers. An old work or winter boot, a woman's old-fashioned high-laced dress boot (which can be obtained at a reasonable price from a used- or vintage-clothing store), clutch bags, and a variety of other flea market or "junk" items can all be fitted with hidden containers that can be filled with water, so only the fresh flowers are seen "growing" out of them. Recycled cans and jars also make interesting flower vases. Emphasize the visual beauty of an arrangement displayed in a clear glass jar or vase by placing a few drops of food coloring in the water; coordinate the water color with the flower colors.

As you arrange your fresh flowers, experiment with the juxtaposition of the blossoms as they rest together in the container. You may notice a fascinating, striking, or eye-pleasing contrast that you can later replicate in your own garden by bringing the two plants together.

Edible flowers (such as roses, pot marigolds, violets, scented geraniums, pansies, and nasturtiums), herb flowers (such as borage, chive, hyssop, mustard blossom, and thyme), and fruit and vegetable flowers (such as apple blossoms, squash and zucchini blossoms, and broccoli flowers) can be creatively used in a multitude of ways in the kitchen: to add unusual colors to salads, to make an attractive bed for appetizers, to decorate a pat of butter or a scoop of sorbet, to top a fruit gelatin mold, to decorate a summer cake, or to use as a simple but attractive garnish for a summer supper. Edible flowers can also make a unique and colorful splash in summer drinks when frozen in ice cubes. To make such ice flowers, first pluck the blossoms from the stems and wash the flowers in lukewarm water. Carefully place each blossom in an individual ice-cube compartment that has been half-filled with water. Since the flowers will float to the surface of the water, freeze the tray of half-filled compartments, then remove from the freezer and add more water to fill each compartment, thus freezing the flowers in the center of the ice cubes.

In your creativity quest for fresh plants, be sure not to overlook some of the more common flowers, herbs, or even weeds. The lowly **dandelion** (*Taraxacum officinale*), which is by far the most easily identifiable wildflower and, as well, the most detested and noxious weed known to suburban lawn-and-garden lovers, was once the darling of American society because of its many virtues. From root to flower, every part of a fresh dandelion was deemed useful. From its apothecary, culinary, and brewery uses of the past to its more recent contributions to the production of rubber from its latex, the dandelion is still considered to be a tasty salad green; a cookable vegetable; an herbal flavoring; a laxative; a restorative; a rich source of vitamins (it has twenty-five times more vitamin A than tomato juice as well as iron, potassium, calcium, and magnesium); an adequate substitute for coffee (from its roasted roots); a satisfying medium-dry white wine with a fresh, light flavor; and the main ingredient in a number of New England colony beverages, including a sweet, lager-flavored summer drink known as Dandelion One-Month Brew.

- -

ANCESTRAL NATURAL CREATIVITY CHALLENGE:

DANDELION ONE-MONTH BREW

This is a fun project to begin on a sunny summer day—the perfect time for gathering the main ingredient, dandelion flowers. Select only opened buds; discard any partially seeded flowers or unopened buds. Separate the flowers from the stalks, but leave the green sepals on. Read over the following instructions, then assemble the ingredients:

> *5 cups of dandelion flowers*
> *½ gallon water*
> *2 pounds of sugar (or an equivalent amount of honey*
> *   or maple syrup for sweetening)*
> *the pared rind and juice of 2 lemons*
> *mint or lemon balm sprigs for garnish*
> *double thickness muslin or cheesecloth for straining*

Wash the dandelion flowers in a colander. Drain thoroughly, then place in an earthenware or plastic container that can be covered with a well-fitting lid or heavy dinner plate. Bring the water to a boil, then pour the boiling water over the dandelions. Cover and let stand for twelve hours.

Strain the liquid through the muslin or cheesecloth into a large saucepan. Add the sugar and pared rind and juice of the lemons. Heat gently—do not bring to a boil—and stir until the sugar (or sweetener) has completely dissolved. Strain the liquid into heat-resistant containers to cool. When the liquid has cooled, transfer into clean, dry glass bottles with strong screw caps or corks. Store upright in a cool place. The brew, which is mildly alcoholic and has a light lager flavor, is ready to drink in three to four weeks.

There are countless other ways to use your natural creativity with fresh flowers, herbs, and grasses.

• Adorn an ordinary basket—or a picnic basket—with wildflowers and flowering herbs simply by inserting the stems of the fresh plants into the weavings of the basket.

• Dress up cloth dinner napkins with a napkin-ring sprig of fresh ivy, wildflowers, or herbs.

• Make a colorful wreath or decorative table centerpiece by tying together stalks of tall grasses and then forming the resulting thick clump into a circle. Bind the two ends securely together to create a circular shape. Then weave the stems of wildflowers, flowering herbs, fresh ivy, lichen, and mosses into the grasses.

• Create a fresh flower necklace. Gather and then tie together the stems of a variety of wildflowers to form a festive garland.

• Prepare your own perfume by first collecting the leaves of fresh, aromatic herbs (such as mint), scented flower blossoms (such as lilac), and scented fresh fruits (such as lemon). Crush and/or mince the leaves, blossoms, and fruits, then mix together. Place the mixture into a container, cover with water, and let sit overnight. The clear juice can then be transferred into decorated glass baby-food jars or other interesting containers and used for up to three or four days.

DRIED PLANTS

Dried plants, also known as everlastings, can be used in much the same manner as fresh plants in a wide variety of naturally creative projects—to make wreaths, floral displays, centerpieces, aromatic sachets, garlands, and so on, as well as to season a variety of recipes—but they must first be preserved through drying. Once dried, the plants will keep for a long time (although they are not, in reality, ever-lasting), so whatever you create with them will look like new from week to week and month to month.

Besides increasing the life of the plant, another benefit to drying the fresh flowers, herbs, and weeds that you collect is being able to store your natural raw materials until you have both the time and the inclination to work with them. This means that you can enjoy the good-weather months outdoors, harvesting and then drying what you gather, and then, when the weather prevents you from going outdoors and you have more free time, you can explore your natural creativity with the ample store of supplies you have on hand.

Fresh plants can be dried in a number of ways. Experiment with each drying process. You may discover interesting differences in the appearance of particular plants, depending on the process you use. Plants are sufficiently dry when their stems snap and the plant feels stiff to the touch.

Air drying (for flowers, herbs, and weeds). Tie the foliage together in small, loose bundles with twine. Ten or twelve stems are enough for a bundle; a handful is too much. Bunch only one species of plant together, and keep the flowers or pods from pressing against one another. Some plants do better hung upside down; others dry best on a drying rack with frequent turning, which prevents the leaves from curling; still others, such as grasses, air dry well if simply stood upright in a container. Some grasses do respond well to the hanging method, including barley, beach grass, crab grass, marsh grass, orchard grass, sorghum, and wheat. Artemisia ("Silver King"), baby's breath, bee balm, blue sage, caspia, cockscomb, coneflowers, feverfew, hydrangea, larkspur, lemon verbena, love-in-a-mist, mint, oregano, statice, strawflowers, sweet Annie, and yarrow are all good candidates for hanging. To maintain the natural curves of vines, such as clematis, or to protect delicate flowers that naturally hang down from stems, such as Chinese lanterns, air dry by hooking the plant materials over a line of string or twine stretched horizontally.

Warmth, dryness, and good ventilation are essential conditions for air drying. The room in which the plants are dried should be dark, because sunlight fades the natural color of the flowers as well as breaks down the chlorophyll in culinary herbs, thereby destroying their flavor. The best place to hang plant materials is in an attic; the next best, a large closet. Be protective of your plant material as well as creative with your air-drying method; you can even dry plant materials through the seat or back of a cane chair. Most flowers and foliage will take three to five weeks to dry. Once dry, they can remain hanging or air drying until ready to use.

Microwaving (for certain flowers and herbs). Place a small amount of foliage on a plain white paper towel. Cover with another paper towel. Place in the microwave, then dry on low power for one to three minutes. Plant material that dries particularly well in the microwave includes calendula, lamb's ears, and marigolds.

Pressing (for flowers, herbs, and weeds with flowers that lie flat and have thin, lightweight blossoms; also, fern fronds). Cut flowers for pressing just before they fully mature, when they are at their peak color. Gather plants on a dry, sunny day, after the dew has evaporated from the leaves and petals and the blossoms are free from moisture. Snip the flowers off the stems, then cut the stems and any foliage, such as the leaves, that you also want to press. Press each item separately; reassemble later on, if desired. Trim large flower clusters so the flowers will lie flat when pressing. Large flower clusters can also be separated into individual florets; press them separately, then reassemble later on to form the flower.

Pressing techniques vary. Some people like to hike the countryside with a knife or small pair of scissors and a pocket-sized book and begin the pressing process while out in the wild. Later on, after returning home, these prepressed materials can be transferred into large books (such as telephone books, encyclopedias, or dictionaries), and then weighted down. Allow about five days for small, thin flowers to be pressed and up to two weeks or longer for large, many-petaled flowers. Take a peek at the flowers every few days to check for signs of moisture and to ensure plants are not sticking to the surface of the paper; if damp, transfer them to the dry pages of another weighted book.

You can also purchase a plant press or make your own. Cut two ½-inch pieces of plywood to the same size—9 x 12 or 12 x 17 are sizes that can accommodate a variety of good-size plant materials. Place sheets of newsprint above and under materials to be pressed to absorb moisture; insert corrugated cardboard sheets, cut to fit the size of the press, between newspaper layers to act as ventilators. Finally, wrap straps or belts tightly around the outside of the boards to hold the press together or drill holes and use wing nuts to apply pressure. Weight the boards with a heavy object, but still check on the plant materials and their moisture content every day or so.

Pressed plant materials can then be removed from the press and stored in envelopes or small boxes until ready for use in any number of craft projects, including creating nature gift tags, stationery, and notecards; for decorating picture frames or mirrors; for decoupage activities; for pressed-plant pictures; for making nature placemats and nature bookmarks; and so on.

Sand drying (for flowers and flower-topped herbs and weeds). This method is ideal for preserving flowers that have more intricate petals, such as tulips, roses, and delphinium. Fill a box half full of clean, dry sifted sand. (Do not use sand from the seashore. It not only contains salt and other minerals that will affect the color of the dried plant material, but also should never be removed from where it is needed the most). Cut the stem of each plant to the right length so that when the stem is inserted in the sand, it is buried up to the base of the flower. (Long stalks of plant material can be placed lengthwise in the box; sift sand in and around individual blossoms to ensure flowers on each side of the stalk are not crushed or flattened.) Gently sprinkle sand over the flowers and in between petals until they are covered completely, up to a depth of one inch. Leave the box in a dry place for two weeks. Then pour out the top sand and carefully ease the flowers and stems out.

Sand baking (for flowers and flower-topped weeds). Fill a baking dish or pan with one to two inches of clean, dry sifted sand. Separate the flowers from the stems, then place the flowers face down in the sand. Carefully pour another inch of sand over the flowers. Bake in a 200° oven for about two hours. Remove from oven and allow to cool. Gently pour off the sand. Lay the flowers on a piece of paper for about an hour, then store face down in a cardboard box. (Note: Drying times may vary from flower to flower. Check on the condition of your flowers 45 minutes into the cooking time. If the flowers look damp or droopy, they need more baking time; if they look dark or dull, they have baked too long and should be removed. Flowers that have been baked to perfection look nearly the same as before they were baked. For future reference, note baking times for a particular species of flower, herb, or weed.)

Sand-substitute materials. To replicate sand drying when sand is not available, substitute a mixture of five pounds of yellow cornmeal to 15 ounces of powdered borax, which is sold in supermarkets. Use a wooden, cardboard, or plastic container for drying (not metal), then follow the instructions given for sand drying. After the plant materials have been dried, the borax-and-meal mixture can be dried for an hour in a 150° oven, stored in an airtight container, and used again.

Silica gel is an effective drying agent that works best for fully open flowers. The small blue crystals absorb moisture from the drying flowers and turn pink; after drying, the gel can be placed in a 150° oven until it regains its original blue color, and then used again. Other plant drying chemicals, or commercial desiccants, have been made from some form of silica gel, but their popularity is on the wane as greater numbers of craftspeople seek more natural methods of preserving plant materials.

The glycerin method is a popular preservative used by florists that works best with evergreen foliage that has been gathered after the new-growth tips have become woody. Bark is stripped from the bottom of the stems. The stem ends are cross-split, and then plunged into a mixture of one cup glycerin and two cups boiling water. The leaves gradually change color as the glycerin slowly seeps into their veins. Magnolia leaves turn milk-chocolate brown, for example; rhododendron leaves take on a deep bronze sheen; and ivy becomes a deeper green. Full absorption of the mixture occurs in about five days, after which time the plant material can be hung upside down in a dark attic or closet for three days to complete the curing process.

❧

Some dried-in-the-field plant materials are ready for use, as is, right after they have been harvested in the late fall, early winter, or even midwinter. This includes goldenrods, grasses, steeplebush, cornstalks, and teasel; but there are many others that can be found along roadsides, fields, gardens, pastures, and even your own back-yard. Cut the stems of these plants; then turn upside down and shake out any seeds before you carry the plants home. As the snow melts and the ground softens, the seeds will have a chance to germinate in the spring, thus replenishing the supply of plant materials.

Even if you live in the city and lack transportation for country-side forages for natural raw materials, you can establish a good business relationship with a florist who offers a wide and interesting selection and who is willing to order in-season plants such as strawflowers for you, which you can then later air dry in your apartment. There is also a surprising number of interesting grasses and weeds in vacant lots and around the edges of buildings and parking lots that can be freely picked without harming the environment.

FRUITS AND VEGETABLES

Perhaps the most common way of creatively using fresh and/or dried fruits and vegetables gathered from the garden or out in the wild involves preparing them in some way for consumption—by drying them, baking them, grilling them, steaming them, smoking them, boiling them, broiling them, roasting them, toasting them, mashing them, pureeing them, blanching them, fermenting them, frying them, or freezing them.

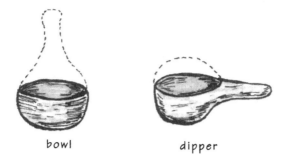

bowl   dipper

Gourd containers, with original shapes

But America's early ancesters also discovered many other uses for cultivated wild edibles. **Gourds**, which grew in various sizes, shapes, and colors, were pierced at both ends at maturity, then turned and wiped daily to keep accumulated moisture away from their surface for a total of three weeks before being put to a variety of good uses. Oftentimes the shape of the gourd determined what its use would be—bottle, dipper, pipe, or powder horn, for instance. The large, round pumpkin gourd, once dried and with its top cut off and seeds removed, made a splendid bowl. Long-handled, dipper-shaped gourds scooped water out of a deep barrel, stream, or spring; ladled soups and stews; and measured ingredients for recipes. Round, short-handled gourds had a small hole cut near their tops and then were hung on walls to store seeds for spring planting. Bottle-shaped gourds, with their slender necks and large, flat-bottomed and bulbous hollow bases, made fine flasks after the top was cut off (a corn cob was used as a stopper); smaller bottle gourds became posy holders. Cymling gourds were converted into baby rattles by cutting a hole in the top and then inserting a handle to fill the hole; the dried seeds that were left inside made considerable noise as they struck against the thin shell. Small gourds were made into ceremonial necklaces and other fashion accessories.

Squash and pumpkins had utilitarian duties as well. The crook-neck, pattypan, and acorn varieties of squash were often arranged in a basket to make a decorative table centerpiece until the squash were ready to be cooked. After the pulp of a large pumpkin had been scraped out for cooking, its shell was often sun-dried to make a decorative bowl; the shell turned an interesting mottled orange color after all the moisture had evaporated.

Besides being eaten raw and cooked, many vegetables and fruits were also used to make natural dyes for fabrics. Here are a few of the colors that can be made from cultivated and in-the-wild natural raw materials by boiling for several minutes in water and then using the tinted water as dye:

- beets—reddish purple
- blackberries, after the seeds are removed—blue
- dandelion roots—bright light purple
- onionskins—either yellow (from yellow onionskins) or red (from red onionskins)
- raspberries—dark red
- spinach—yellow green
- strawberries—light pinkish red

Corn was probably the edible most utilized by America's early settlers. By the time Christopher Columbus had set sail on his infamous voyage of 1492, two to three hundred varieties of corn had already been developed in America, including the common yellow and white varieties with which you are familiar today as well as blue, pink, purple, black, red, and even variegated varieties. Some varieties even boasted different colors of tassels, leaves, silk, and cobs; in fact, it was the job of certain men in a tribe to propagate seeds for specific colors year after year, in search not just for a particular flavor or texture but, as well, for the color that would increase that person's standing within the tribal community.

Native Americans used every part of the **corn** plant—the stalk, shucks, kernels, cob, and silk. Because corn could sustain whole populations throughout the long winter months, corn became sacred; it was, in fact, the basis of many religious ceremonies. Each year, for instance, the Seneca Indians participated in marathon dances to offer thanks to the Great Spirit for the grain. The Pilgrims and the early settlers at Jamestown sur-

Sweet corn.   Flint corn.

vived their first year in America because of corn; corn thus became indispensable to them as well as to all their descendants and to numerous other groups that later settled in America. Pioneers ate and stored the corn; fed the green stalks and kernels to horses, pigs, chickens, and cows; burned the cobs for fuel; braided the husks into sun bonnets, footwear, chair seats, and floor mats; stuffed mattresses; made the famous corncob pipes; converted stalks into musical instruments; and made dolls from both the cobs and shucks of corn.

ANCESTRAL NATURAL CREATIVITY CHALLENGE:

CORNCOB DOLL

A corncob doll is made from a dried cob of corn. Some corncobs, such as Indian corn, have dried kernels in a variety of colors on them; these can be used to add color to your doll. But corn cobs that have kernels removed can be just as interesting to work with and look at.

Here's how to make a corncob doll:

• Glue strands of dried corn silk for hair to the blunt (not pointed) end of the cob or use another dried natural plant material that would suggest hair.

• Tie a strip of corn husk around the corn about two inches from the top of the head (blunt end) to form a neck scarf.

• Use your imagination to create facial features between the hair and the neck scarf. For example, embed peppercorns or cloves in the kernel holes to suggest eyes; a cut corn kernel to suggest a nose; pine needles or other dried materials to suggest the mouth.

• To make a corncob man, split the cob up the center about three inches from the pointed end to form legs. Fashion a pair of overalls out of scrap fabric; make other accessories out of rags or natural raw materials.

• To make a corncob woman, make a dress out of scrap fabric. Wrap around the doll and tie at the waist with a grass belt, or slit a hole in the top of a circle of fabric and slip over the doll's head. Cinch at the waist with an all-natural belt.

You can experiment with and discover dozens of other ways to make creative use out of some of nature's most common gifts from the wild countryside—gifts that you probably take for granted because they are there all the time, sometimes without your even noticing them. Poke around your backyard, look around you on your commute to work, or visit a nearby pasture. Open your eyes and take notice of the interesting plants that grow persistently, beautifully, and deliciously all around you.

Exercising Your Natural Creativity in the Wild Countryside

1. Explore some of the many uses of one of the more common and fragrant flowers—and cousin of the popular apple—the rose. Several varieties of wild roses thrive throughout the United States, often forming thickets along streams, roadsides, fences, open woods, and meadows. The rose hip, or seed pod of the rose, which grows from the flowers, is usually pink, white, or red. Just a few rose hips reportedly have as much vitamin C as a single orange. In fact, during World War II, five million pounds of rose hips were gathered from roadsides to take the place of then-scarce citrus fruits, which are notorious for preventing scurvy. Rose hips can be eaten off the bushes, cut up in salad, baked in cake or bread, or boiled into jam or jelly. You can also use the petals of the rose to make a tasty tea or a refreshing toilet water. To make rose water, simply boil a cup of water with a cup of pink and/or red rose petals. Boil for one minute, then cover and let cool. The petals will tint the water to a rosy color during the cooling process. Strain the liquid through a sieve to remove the petals; store in a decorative bottle or glass jar. Splash on as a toilet water, add to a bath, or use as a facial astringent. Although the rose water lasts for just a few days, it is not only easy to brew, but also makes a nice gift.

2. Make a kitchen wreath out of fresh herbs. Collect the sprigs of a wide range of fresh herbs—red and green basil, rosemary, parsley, mint, dill, oregano, sage, and so on. Fashion a hoop out of a thin, green stick, then tie the ends securely together. Use green yarn to

bind the stems of a few sprigs of different herbs together in order to make an interesting arrangement; tie the arrangement securely to the hoop. Continue tying bunches of herbal arrangements to the hoop in the same direction. Then hang in the kitchen and use during cooking, even after the herbs have dried.

3. Find a small piece of dried, decorative wood, interesting in shape and flat enough to rest securely on a table. Scoop or scrape out a fairly shallow depression in the wood. Fill this area with living mosses. Water sparingly every few days to keep the moss green. Or assemble a collection of small pieces of wood, scoop out shallow depressions, fill with some dirt or potting soil, and plant herb seeds for an indoor wild garden.

4. Make your own naturally creative nature wrapping paper for a gift you are planning to give. Purchase a roll of plain brown wrapping paper, or use a paper grocery bag. Wrap the gift. Then, using glue and your pressed plant materials, decorate the paper.

5. Use some of the larger pressed plants you have made to create ink prints for nature art prints or stationery. Lay a single pressed plant material on a folded sheet of newspaper. Roll a hard rubber roller first in printer's ink, then over the plant material until it is covered with the ink. Gently lift the inked material off the newspaper, then place ink side down onto the paper on which you wish to make a print. Lay a sheet of clean paper on top of the material, then press down hard on the inked material with a rolling pin, being careful not to move the plant material. Gently lift the paper and inked material to see the results.

6. Create a dried herb-and-spice sachet with fragrant flora such as rose petals, lavender, eucalyptus, cinnamon sticks, and citrus peels. Crumble the materials together, then place them in a small muslin bag. Store in a closet or dresser drawer. Or crumble these fragrant items together into a pan of water; bring to a boil to create an all-natural, aromatic home air freshener.

7. County and state agricultural fairs are excellent sources for collecting sheaves of grain, straw, hay, and other dried grasses. Simply ask the farmers if you can have a small sample after they display their grain for judging; they usually throw it away anyway. Dry the grain stalks on newspapers indoors or outside in the full sun (for a lighter color), turning them occasionally to prevent mold. You can

make a simple straw wreath, hanging mobiles, straw figures, and Christmas tree ornaments with just a little glue—and a lot of creative energy!

8. Fill slender glass vials with colored sand or stones (which can be purchased at a hobby or pet store that sells fish tank supplies). Insert a contrasting-colored sprig of a dried flower, herb, or weed into the sand for a simple, yet elegant display.

9. Have fun expressing your natural creativity by carving a jack-o'-lantern out of a pumpkin during Halloween season. Or, instead of carving the pumpkin, use the empty shell as a soup tureen for a fall or winter dinner party. (Try to locate a recipe for pumpkin soup to create the greatest effect with the natural tureen.) You can also wash and dry the seeds to prepare a great-tasting and nutritious natural snack—toasted pumpkin seeds. Mix enough salad oil or melted butter, soy sauce, and garlic powder together in a bowl to lightly coat the dry seeds. Then spread the seeds on a cookie sheet, place in a 325° oven, and bake until golden brown. Periodically reposition seeds while baking so the seeds toast evenly.

10. Gather a supply of dried cornstalks from a local farm or farm stand. Then experiment with creating a variety of cornstalk ornaments for a Christmas tree, mobile, or window display. Can you make a bird out of a corn shuck? An angel? A butterfly? A spider? A bat? Use your everlastings to decorate your finished crafts; rub the cornstalks with ripe berries to add natural color.

5

WILDLIFE:
Natural Creativity from Living Creatures

. . . Before they (the French) came, did we not live better than we do. . . ? In what respect, then, had we occasion for them? Was it for their guns? The bows and arrows which we used, were sufficient to make us live well. Was it for their white, blue, and red blankets? We can do well enough with buffalo skins, which are warmer; our women wrought feather blankets for the winter, and mulberry mantles for the summer. . . .

—STUNG SERPENT (Natchez) ca. 1720

October 1540: The Cacique (chief) was at home, in a piazza . . . the Indians of the highest rank being nearest to his person. One of them shaded him from the sun with a circular umbrella, spread wide, the size of a target, with a small stem, and having deerskin extended over cross-sticks quartered with red and white, which at a distance make it took of taffeta, the colors were so very perfect.

—Recorded by a Portugese knight in his journal, upon encountering native royalty at Tascaluza (central Alabama)

. . . He was deep in thought and did not notice, perched at the top-most point in the pinery, the Great White Eagle. . . . Under the bird's keen eyed scouting protection Dekanawideh's "great idea" evolved itself into specific form. Drafting a plan as he sat on the grass, trusting merely to his memory did not prove satisfactory.

Taking an eagle feather, placing it upon the ground, "That," he said, "shall represent the great idea. . . ."

—JOHN OJIJATEKHA BRANT-SERO, Mohawk historian, 1901

(Excerpts from *The Native Americans: An Illustrated History*, by David Hurst Thomas et al.)

Native Americans had countless great ideas when it came to creatively, functionally, and, after white settlers had begun to impact upon Indian society, economically crafting from the wildlife with which they shared their lands. The bounties from any successful hunt were seemingly endless, and far exceeded the sustenance that could be obtained from the meat. The animals were *everything* to the Native Americans: to them, to their daily life, and to their way of life. The tools the Indians used to ensure their survival—such integral implements as scrapers, knives, and awls—were fashioned out of animal bones, tusks, horns, and antlers. A large animal's ribs, when tied together with rawhide, made a winter sled or a three-season travois. Animal furs and hides provided the people with fabrics from which they fashioned essential clothing as well as elaborate and symbolic ceremonial attire. Furs and hides were also shaped into warm and protective footwear and blankets; coveted calfskins gently cradled newborns in soft swaddling. The large, tough hides of full-grown animals were sewn together to construct a snug, water-tight **tipi** or wigwam big enough to shelter an entire family. Smaller hides were put to use in making drums. The neck pelts of large animals such as buffalo were used to make shields as well as bull boats, or single-person kayaks. Animal sinew was stretched, dried, and used as strong cordage and thread. Both horns and hair went into the making of headdresses. Animal tails decorated lodges. Claws and teeth were woven into necklaces, dresses, and robes. Hooves and scrota were transformed into ceremonial rattles. Medicine men valued a variety of animal body parts in their potions and prescriptions: an animal bladder became a medicine bag; an animal tail, a medicine switch. The skull, too, was set aside for use in prayers and ceremonial rituals designed to pay tribute to the beast and to entice that particular animal to return again.

Plains buffalo hide tipi

Marine wildlife was also put to good use by the Native Americans. Shells became digging tools, drinking cups, clothing decorations, jewlery, or even wampum—a means of exchange. Exquisite carvings were etched on bone, tusks, and shells. Game dice, beads, and toys were made from bone. Sharks' teeth were displayed in ceremonial attire.

All creatures great and small provided valuable natural materials for the Native Americans in ways that extended well beyond the dinner table. And the same held true for the country's earliest settlers, who initially learned from and relied upon Indian ingenuity before metals and man-made materials replaced the crude but effective Indian implements and the laborious crafting that went into their exquisite and intricate design work.

Even though North American explorers had returned to their homelands with amazing stories of a land in which birds were numerous beyond belief, the early American settlers were still astounded when the sky darkened from the thousands of passenger pigeons that flew overhead or when wild ducks and geese covered entire surfaces of ponds and lakes. Huge flocks of peasant, quail, and grouse thundered up from the tall grasses wherever they walked, and native songbirds displayed brilliant flashes of color against the lush, forest-green backdrop. After the settlers observed the plumed headdresses of Indian chieftains and the Native American garments that were skillfully and beautifully adorned with feathers sewn on hides, the settlers began to see the numerous birds as being functional as well as succulent. Wild birds such as the turkey, duck, goose, and pigeon were thus domesticated, valued not just for their meat but for their feathers as well. Soft breast feathers filled bed ticks and coverlets; light, fluffy down was prized for pillows. The long, hard quills from geese were converted into writing instruments; their large wing feathers became paintbrushes. Pheasant plumage, along with the red and blue tail feathers of cardinals, made beautiful as well as functional household dusters. Turkey wings swept ashes off the hearth.

During the colonial period in America, the creation of feather pictures became all the rage for settlers; the plucked plumage of pheasant, grouse, and songbirds was glued on paper or thin strips of wood to create fanciful and colorful birds and animals for display. Fluffy flowers were also made from pin feathers by bunching and tying them together in a miniature version of a feather duster. During the eighteenth century, after chickens became quite common in America, there was never a shortage of on-hand raw materials for making feather-flower creations, for nearly every small town home had its henhouse, and most city dwellers bought their supper chickens live and then dressed them at home. When ingenious homemakers discovered that chicken feathers could be dyed—this was not true at the time of the plumage of ducks and geese because of the oily coating that helps keep the birds afloat—dyed feather-flower arrangements came into vogue. The completed feather creations, which sometimes consisted of elaborately constructed pyramids of feather flowers, were then placed under bell-shaped glass domes to protect the feathers from the ravages of insects and the damaging effects of air and dust. Further inventive feather-creative discoveries included steaming feathers over a boiling teakettle and then pulling the feathers through the fingers or over a dull knife blade, which resulted in their curling or curving easily, thereby creating more realistic feather flowers.

Later, when John James Audubon's paintings made it fashionable to admire not just the feathers but the whole bird, stuffed birds came into demand as the most-requested home accessory. The more colorful the species, the more desired it was; thus, it was not unusual for an American home to display a stuffed parrot from a South American jungle next to a Rocky Mountain bluebird. A natural habitat was often created to display these stuffed birds; a tree branch on which the bird or birds perched, for example, might be stuck into a bed of dyed, dried moss, which was then placed under a domed glass cover to preserve the specimens.

Initially, the early settlers valued the utilitarian craftings Native Americans made from animals; after all, their survival in the strange new land depended upon the experience and expertise of those who already knew how to survive. Later on, such handcrafts became valued commodities of exchange when the settlers began to interact with the Indians and the two cultures discovered that a vigorous and equitable trade in goods could benefit both parties. A woven Indian blanket might be exchanged for a metal knife, for example, and both the Indians and the settlers would gain a practical object that would assist them in their daily lives.

But it wasn't long before more and more settlers arrived in America, bringing with them items that had been created from raw materials not used by the Indians, and the skills to make more of these items. The colonists set off on their own path of creative exploration to discover ways to ease the difficulties of everyday life and to make mankind less dependent upon and impacted by nature. The peaceful coexistence the settlers had once maintained with the Indians was thus threatened by the emergence of two different sets of philosophies: one that encouraged obtaining greater quantities of raw materials and goods more efficiently and quickly in order to turn a profit as well as gain control over nature, and one that respected nature and drew from it only when necessary. The settlers' impatience showed in their disregard for honoring what the Indians considered to be gifts of nature that had been bestowed upon them. Why wait for the Indians to bring in a few buffalo skins every once in a while, they reasoned, when they could simply load their own firearms and shoot as many of the lumbering beasts as they could? Why wait for the Indians to weave their one-of-a-kind, intricately designed blankets when textile mills and looms could be built that could churn out stacks of the so-called authentic Indian blankets?

To the Indians, the trade goods of the settlers seemed to exist in endless quantities—knives, guns, pots, pans, shirts, blankets, hoes, axes. What the Indians predominantly had to offer in exchange for such things, besides their own handcrafted items, were the pelts of sea otter, beaver, and buffalo. But dwindling numbers from slaughter and the settlers' insatiable lust for amazing quantities of the pelts compromised the Indians' strong spiritual and moral beliefs. Even though the Indians were accustomed to killing for survival, killing for trade was rarely easy for them. Animals were literally life to thousands of Indians, providing them each day with the very basic elements of food, shelter, and clothing. The Indians thus revered the animals and were sickened by the senseless slaughter of such creatures for little more than coveted claws or other body parts that would be used to impress others or to make a fashion statement.

While Indian beliefs and customs with respect to animals varied enormously across America, virtually all Indian peoples regarded animals not as some subordinate order of beings put at the service of humans, but as persons—"other-than-human" persons—with whom human beings established relationships. Because of this, animals were worshipped and revered; Indians made hunting holy because they believed that unless the animals were honored with proper rituals and treated with the utmost respect, the animals would not consent to capture. As long as there was a need to kill an animal, and this need was communicated through proper rituals to the animal being hunted, the Indians were rewarded by the animal's "consent" to its capture.

Too, the Indians had difficulty with the whole concept of trade; they usually traded with the settlers with wonder or with scorn. In reality, the Indians needed the settlers for nothing; everything they had, they reasoned, had been provided for them by the Creator, and their lifestyle, regardless of the tribe, emphasized limited, rather than excessive, wants. The following story, told by Pawnee Curly Chief in 1860, details this philosophy:

> The man who came was from the Government. He wanted to make a treaty with us, and to give us presents, blankets and guns, and flint and steel, and knives.
>
> The Head Chief told him that we needed none of these things. He said, "We have our buffalo and our corn. These things the Ruler gave to us, and they are all that we need. See this robe. This keeps me warm in winter. I need no blanket."
>
> The white man had with him some cattle, and the Pawnee Chief said, "Lead out a heifer here on the prairie." They led her out, and the Chief stepping up to her, shot her through behind the shoulder with his arrow, and she fell down and died. Then the Chief said, "Will not my arrow kill? I do not need your guns." Then he took his stone knife and skinned the heifer, and cut off a piece of fat meat. When he had done this, he said, "Why should I take your knives? The Ruler has given me something to cut with."

Exploring your natural creativity with wildlife today should emphasize first and foremost that you respect the life of all living creatures. Although you may think this goes without saying, especially in light of today's animal rights–conscious society, unless you are a hunter who kills in the way Native Americans once did—to put to good use, in your life or in the lives of others, as much of the animal as possible—trophy hunting of *any* living creature is not exercising your natural creativity. This rule applies to all animals and birds as well as to insects. There are trophy hunters who seek to bag a magnificent beast just to hang over a mantle, as well as craftspeople who seek ivory obtained by poaching, and, surprisingly, lepidopterists (butterfly collectors) who think nothing of illegally collecting endangered and protected butterflies—oftentimes bringing these most exquisitely beautiful specimens closer to the brink of extinction—merely to possess them.

In exercising your natural creativity with all wildlife, always follow the motto shown at the end of any movie in which wildlife has been used during filming: *Harm no creatures.* Also, *bring no harm to creatures.* Where a wild thing lives should never be disturbed unless you are absolutely certain that the home has been abandoned *for good* (never, for your own safety, try to enter or dig into an animal's den) or is, by habit, discarded after a year's use, as some birds' nests are (consult field guides or the National Audubon Society in your area to confirm this first before you remove a nest from the ground or a tree). To avoid diseases and parasites, don't scavenge dead carcasses you come across for body parts—a deer for its antlers, for instance, or a bird for its feathers.

The best way to exercise your natural creativity with wildlife is to make use of the discards of wildlife, better termed wild gifts, which you may be pleasantly surprised to find on your journeys into nature. Such lost-and-found items are rarely discovered intentionally; rather, they usually present themselves when they are ready to be found. Because of this, wild gifts can take on great significance, especially if you regard them, as the Native Americans once did (and still do), as symbols that impart a meaning or message for you or for your life. Most people who have come across a wild gift will hold on to it for years; they can often recount exactly where they found the gift and what was going on for them at that particular time in their lives, thereby revealing the meaning or message that gift had for them.

When placed in creative displays, wild gifts can be used to communicate a creature's "medicine," or its connection to all of life. This medicine can help to develop personal power, strength, and understanding through the essence of the creature, or its totem. For example, an owl feather can symbolize wisdom, and thus impart a reminder to think more deeply about the people, places, and things in your life; the magical colors reflected in a dragonfly's wings, conveying a shifting of color, energy, and form, can symbolize the need for change and growth in your life.

Although you may be tempted to obtain wildlife raw materials from sources such as Indian dealers (who can provide you, for a high fee, with coveted eagle feathers, bear claws, moose antlers, and so on), wholesale milliner's stores (for white turkey, swan, goose, hawk, and owl feathers), craft stores (where plastic bags of dyed feathers are sold, along with bone beads, shark's teeth, and so on), and poultry dealers, you can best discover a wide array of wonderful wildlife gifts whenever you are outdoors, where the wildlife—animals, birds, insects, and countless other creatures—lives. It doesn't matter whether you reside in the country, in the suburbs, or in the city; wherever and whenever you go outdoors, there will always be something wild living nearby; so, too, will there be wild gifts for you to find.

ANIMALS

Animals provide a number of gifts you can find in the wild and use to explore your natural creativity. To discover animal gifts, look for animal "roads," or trails, that have been established by the animals in their travels back and forth to the same places. A typical animal **trail** is a narrow path about six to ten inches wide that meanders through the woods or criss-crosses open fields. As you follow one or more of these trails, it may seem as if you are wandering about aimlessly; animals are renowned for taking the path of least resistance

fox

squirrel

deer

rather than the most direct route, which means that they prefer to go around fallen trees, brush, and other obstacles rather than over them, as humans would. However, the trails usually lead to a specific place of importance for the animals; most lead to food and water, while some are used only in winter or summer, and a few are reserved as escape routes to elude danger.

Because many kinds of animals often share the same trail and because most trails are used for decades—animals, after all, are creatures of habit—once you discover the network of animal roads in a nearby woods or field, you can then travel it frequently to scavenge gifts throughout the year. Pay attention, however, to any new construction, or subtrail extensions off these roads, which may lead to underground dens or shallow depressions on the ground where an animal rests. Although subtrails may be harder to find, what you discover when you locate an animal's resting spot may be quite fascinating.

If you live in or near moose, elk, or deer country, then you have a good chance of finding shed antlers during your walks in the woods. The best antlers are those that have escaped insect or animal destruction after being discarded. When you are lucky enough to find antlers, brush them free of dust and dirt, then bring them home and let them air dry for a few weeks. Antlers can be displayed as is or, if you choose to get more creative, you can convert the antlers into a coat rack, hat rack, or candlestick holder, cut off parts of the antler to form the handle of a coffee mug or the base of a lamp, or even convert the entire antler into a chandelier. (The 1997 sale price of a moose chandelier at the Mangy Moose, a mooseabilia store in Freeport, Maine, was $5,000!)

Besides antlers, other wildlife gifts you may find as you follow animal trails in the woods and across open fields include: tufts of fur and hair that have been shed, scratched loose, left behind after an animal has rubbed its hide on the rough bark of a tree, or that are remnants of a kill; the skulls, bones, teeth, and claws of prey as well as predatory animals (including moles, mice, raccoons, porcupines, and coyote); and wild cat and bear claw markings that have been scratched into the ground and into trees (a rubbing of such markings can be made by laying a piece of paper on top of the markings and then rubbing firmly over the paper with a dark pencil, wax crayon, or piece of charcoal). Other things that are left behind by the animal—its own droppings, for instance—have been and can be creatively used in any number of ways. Dried animal droppings from a large animal, such as a caribou, can be used as campfire starters. A company called Maine Line Products offers jewelry made of lacquered moose droppings.

As you follow animal roads, you may notice the tracks that animals leave behind in the mud, dirt, and snow. Use a guide book to help you identify the animals that made the tracks, or bring along a tracking stick marked with some of the more common animal tracks you may find in your area. Use this stick for reference and, as well, carry a permanent marker so you can draw new tracks on your stick.

Castings can also be made of the animal tracks. Dried castings can be put on display as is, used as paperweights, or painted and then hung on a wall.

ANCESTRAL NATURAL CREATIVITY CHALLENGE:

ANIMAL-TRACKS CASTINGS

Animal tracking is an ancient art that goes back thousands of years. It was a necessary skill for early hunters who, because they lacked such long-distance weaponry as rifles, needed to get as close to an animal as possible without being detected. This lost art of tracking can be rediscovered through sharp eyes and diligence whenever you are out in nature. The tracks that you find can then be easily preserved by making animal-tracks castings.

You will need to carry the following items with you into the woods:

- plaster wall patch or plaster of Paris,
- a small plastic pail (for mixing the plaster),
- several thin, long strips of cardboard (measuring 2 inches wide by 12 to 18 inches long),
- paper clips,
- a canteen or container filled with water,
- a large spoon or stirring stick, and
- rags in which to protectively wrap the finished cast.

Locate an animal track or tracks in mud or firm, wet sand in wooded areas, along paths or in fields, or near streams. Carefully remove any leaves, sticks, or other loose debris in the track(s) without disturbing the print(s). Curve your precut cardboard strips to form a circle around each track you wish to cast. Use the paper clips to hold your strips in place, then carefully press the cardboard circle into the ground around the track.

front   hind

Beaver.

Prepare the plaster according to directions. Pour or spoon the plaster carefully into each animal track, taking care to fill the deepest part first. Allow the plaster to flow into the track and then into the cardboard circle until it reaches about ¼ inch from the top of the cardboard. Smooth the surface of the plaster with the long side of the mixing stick.

Let the plaster dry until hard, which may take anywhere from a half-hour to an hour to even an entire day, depending on the type of plaster you use. (If you wish to leave the area for any length of time, especially if your plaster will take a long time to dry, take along a wire screen to use as a cover to protect the plaster from inquisitive flying or crawling insects or debris that may fall into it from above.) If you are planning to hang your casting, insert a picture wire before the plaster sets.

The plaster is dry when you cannot press your fingerprint into the center of the plaster. Remove the casting carefully from each track as well as from the cardboard circling. Wrap each casting in a rag to protect it during your journey home.

— · — · — · — · — · — · — · — · — · — · — · — · — · — · — · — · — · —

Animal bones, depending on their size, can make beautiful pieces of sculpture when displayed alone, against an interesting background. A large bone, such as a moose pelvic bone that has been bleached white by the sun and wind, looks less like a bone and more like a work of art. Exquisite bones that have been polished to a shine by the elements can be picked up from the desert floor in arid parts of the western United States.

You can also bleach any bones you find yourself; this process is also recommended for bones that need to be cleaned before use. To do so, first drop the bones in a pot of boiling water. Add a small amount of detergent, then simmer until attached tissue and debris loosens from the bone or can easily be loosened with an old toothbrush or stiff scrub brush. For hollow bones, use a bottle brush to remove the soft marrow. Once the bone is clean, soak it overnight in a pot that contains a mixture of ammonia and water. The next day, rinse away the ammonia water and set the bones aside to dry.

If you want to avoid this process of bone cleaning, you can also bury bones in dirt for up to two weeks. Organic materials will then naturally be removed. Or, in the summer, leave bones that need to be cleaned in your backyard; the ants and other insects will love this surprise treat!

Smaller bones with interesting shapes can be converted into bracelets, necklaces, or earrings. Bones can also be decorated with brilliant colors, designs, and/or nature scenes and displayed.

BIRDS

The gifts from birds are much easier to collect. Whether you live in the city, the suburbs, or the country, whenever you step outside you will invariably find a variety of discarded feathers, broken eggshells from hatched baby birds, and birds' nests that have fallen from trees.

Birds' nests are, in and of themselves, a creative decoration that stands alone. Study a nest closely to see what kinds of materials have been creatively employed by the bird to provide a sturdy, warm, and secure shelter for sleeping, resting, and raising a family in a world in which natural nesting materials are rapidly disappearing. There are fantastic stories of quite inventive nests, as described by Jane and Will Curtis in *Backyard Bird Habitat*: a robin once incorporated a ten-dollar bill into her nest, and one particularly creative and determined European redstart used in her nest ". . . 361 stones, 15 nails, 146 pieces of bark, 14 bamboo splinters, 3 pieces of tin, 35 pieces of adhesive tape, 103 pieces of hard dirt, several rags and bones, 1 piece of glass, 4 pieces of inner tubes and, last but not least, 30 pieces of horse manure!"

You can also become a creative consultant to the birds in your neighborhood by helping them decorate their springtime nests. To do so, simply shake a throw rug from your house outdoors or toss a few short pieces of yarn under a nearby tree in the late winter. The following summer or fall, you may be able to examine nests that have been built and will most likely find strands of your own hair, your pet's hair, lint and threads from your clothing, and the pieces of yarn you made available woven into the nests. Birds couldn't care less whether their nests are lined with spider-egg casings and bark fibers or Christmas-tree icicles and whatever drops out of your wallet.

Before you take any abandoned or fallen bird's nest indoors, first make sure that it is free of insects, decay, and dampness. Then set it by itself on a windowsill or table, display it on a branch hung on a wall, position it on an indoor tree plant, or use it to create an interesting centerpiece for the dining room table. You may also use a bird's nest as a storage space for any eggshells or feathers that you find.

Bird feathers can be used in a variety of creative ways: in mobiles made entirely out of small twigs and bird feathers; in unique ornamental jewelry; in bird sculptures created out of pinecones and other forest materials (use the feathers as wings on your sculptures); in woodland wreaths; in an Indian warbonnet or headdress; and so on. However, the best way to use any feather follows nature's way—by hanging the feather in the wind. The wind not only restores tired-looking feathers but gives you an opportunity to see firsthand the natural ingenuity of flight.

Bird feathers come in three types: **flight, down,** and **contour**. The flight feather has a stiff, hollow central shaft running its entire length, with crisp fibers on opposite sides of the shaft. Down feathers have very short, pliable shafts and wispy feather fibers. The contour feather is a smooth,

contour

down

flight

Bird feathers

surface feather that streamlines the bird and is colored and patterned to contribute to the coloration of the bird.

Because a feather is both fragile and indestructible under most ordinary conditions, most found feathers can be washed with warm, sudsy water and then spread on towels or newspaper to dry. More often than not, crumpled-looking feathers can be restored simply by rubbing the web with the fingers. If this fails, hold the feather for a few moments over the steaming spout of a boiling teakettle, and then rub it again with your fingers.

Many other wildlife gifts await your walks in the woods, across the countryside, along rivers and streams, and through city parks. Dead bugs, butterflies, and moths—if found in good condition—can be used in any natural display. Abandoned wasp and bee nests, fascinating in their durability as well as their lightweight, paper-thin, and seemingly fragile construction, can be displayed as is or sprayed with shellac and then used as a base in which to display dried weeds.

Common garden spider

Even a **spider** web, with its lovely pattern, can be viewed as a wonderous piece of natural artwork in itself. It can also be used to create interesting web art. Hunt for uninhabited spider webs outdoors on a calm day. Take along with you black construction paper, talcum powder, and hairspray or shellac spray. When you find a web that is fairly intact, sprinkle first with powder. Then carefully lift the web with the paper until the web breaks free and is stuck to the paper. Spray the web lightly with the hairspray or shellac; your print may be so interesting that you'll want to frame it.

❦

Wildlife gifts are exciting discoveries that can give you the merest of glimpses and the tiniest of revelations into a hidden world—a world of wild creatures that are living day after day in the wild. Whenever you are fortunate enough to be presented with any gifts from these exotic creatures, appreciate first what they are made of rather than what you can make of them. Sometimes the most naturally creative way to use any wildlife gift is just to look at it—

to marvel at the wonder of its mere existence. As American nature writer Edwin Way Teale once observed, "One vivid memory remains of passing through the city. A small boy, five or six at most, had picked up a dead monarch butterfly from a pile of litter beside the street. He was standing entranced, bending forward, oblivious to all around him. It seemed as though I were looking at myself when young. A door was opening for him, a door beyond which lay all the beauty and mystery of nature."

Exercising Your Natural Creativity with Wildlife

1. Create a deck of Wildlife Medicine cards. Using heavy stock cardboard, cut a bunch of uniformly sized cards. On each card, draw a picture of each wildlife gift you discover on your journeys out into nature: a feather, a bird's nest, an animal track, a tuft of fur, a dead butterfly, a bee or wasp nest, discarded antlers, a bone, shed snake skin, an abandoned spider's web, a cracked eggshell, and so on. Identify the gift (if you can), tell where and when you found it, and then think about what message, or medicine, the gift conveys to you. Consult these cards on a regular basis to discover your personal power or to gain insight in your life by calling on the power of a card: randomly select a card and then reflect on what you can learn from that creature's wild essence.

2. With a handsaw, cut a coaster-size piece of wood from one of your forest-floor branch or log drops. With a block cutting or wood-burning tool (available in craft stores), either cut or burn into the wood an animal track. Shellac and/or stain the finished coaster. Make a set of four coasters that depicts the tracks of a variety of animals and/or birds, then give as gifts.

3. Prepare a map that displays your "creative foraging" area. On your map, sketch and label topographical details such as hills and valleys; specific sites such as ponds and rivers; trail, animal "road," and animal subtrail routes; wild-gift locale particulars such as "Where I found a coyote print," "Where I located several owl feathers," "Where there is a wasps' nest"; and so on. Add to your map to refine details or whenever you discover something new.

4. Collect a large number of different feathers from different

birds. A good source of feathers can be found near a lake or river, where waterfowl nest, preen, and molt on the banks. Then experiment with what you can do to the feathers to add variety to your feather crafts. Find out what happens when the feathers are dipped in paint . . . in food coloring . . . in tea or coffee . . . soaked with water . . . sprayed with paint or shellac . . . steamed over a teakettle . . . bent . . . cut with scissors . . . and so on. Use what you discover to create interesting arrangements with your feathers.

5. Create a woodland wreath out of leaves, dried lichens and mosses, acorns and seed pods, nuts, twigs, feathers, and fur. Strive for subtle contrasts of both textures and colors.

6. Visit a Native American crafts show. Ask the craftspeople how they collect their wildlife crafting materials today. Find out which items are the most prized and/or the hardest to find. Learn what substitutes they use when they cannot obtain wildlife materials traditionally used in the creation of a handcraft.

7. If you are not rewarded with the discovery of wild bones on your nature forays, steal a bone from your dog or buy bones from a butcher or meat market. Prepare the bones in the same way as you would a bone found in the wild. Then experiment with what you can do with the bone. Will your knife cut or chip the bone? How can you break the bone without any tools? Can you sketch on the bone or make designs in any other way on its surface? Could you make a musical instrument out of the bone?

8. Make your own version of an arrow from a straight stick, an arrow point, and one or more found feathers.

9. Study one of the spider web art prints you created. Then, using a drop branch with an interesting shape as a "base," try to replicate the intricate pattern with brightly colored yarn, quilting threads, thin strips of leather, or jeweler's wire.

10. Create a wreath of bird-nesting materials, then hang outdoors in late winter. Observe the birds that come to the wreath and the types of materials they collect. At the start of the summer, find out what remains—if anything—on your bird-nest wreath.

6

WILD EDGE:
Seaside Natural Creativity

There is a perpetual mystery and excitement in living on the seashore, which is in part a return to childhood...the child sees the bright shells, the vivid weeds and red sea anemones of the rock pools with wonder and with the child's eye for minutiae. . . — Scottish nature writer GAVIN MAXWELL

I have a seashell collection; maybe you've seen it? I keep it scattered on beaches all over the world. — American comedian STEVEN WRIGHT

SEASHELLS ARE, BY FAR, the greatest raw material for natural creativity that can be found at the "wild edges" of America—the beautiful, vocal, ever changing, tumultuous seashores. But these **beaches** also offer so much more. Second after second, day after day, the waves race from the shore and back into the ocean to retrieve an incredible amount of interesting items from the water, which they then drop, like dutiful puppies, right at your feet. There are shells of all sizes and shapes—some are so small that they look like grains of sand; some are so large that they could be used as planters—and each has its own distinctive appearance, unique design, and soft color. There are pieces of driftwood—sometimes created out of worm-eaten boards, sometimes out of the trunks and roots of trees. There are pebbles worn so smooth that they look like precious gems. There are skulls of shorebirds as well as their

Outer dune

feathers, crustacean carcasses, and the jawbones of fish and ocean mammals. There are a variety of seaweeds. There are "civilized" objects that are carried out by the waves or lost at sea and later return from their ocean voyage with a new, weathered look: sharp shards of broken glass polished into smooth, soft-toned sun-and-surf stained glass; children's toys remade into interesting sea sculptures; buoy nets and lobster-trap markers converted into coveted castaways for a nautical collection. And there are lots of other treasures as well: strange and fascinating objects whose point of origin is unknown— all sorts of mysterious flotsam and jetsam that come to rest on the sandy beaches, lying scattered about like clues to some sort of mind-boggling mystery at sea.

And then there is the sand—tons and tons of sand, some as soft as silk, some as coarse as sandpaper, some white, some pink, some black, some grey. Sand, the raw material of beaches and, as well, the end product of erosion of these same beaches, is made and remade generation after generation by three things: wind, water, and the erosion of rocks, gemstones, minerals, broken shells, and the crumbled exoskeletons of marine animals. Most North American beaches contain sand made up of 90 percent quartz, which is a major component of granite, the earth's most plentiful rock. Gemstones such as garnet and topaz are also found on any beach, in bits measuring from the size of a pin point to that of a lead pencil. (In fact, parts of Fire

Island, New York, turn nearly blood-red in winter when strong winds scour the beach of its fine top layer of light sand, thereby exposing the underlying heavy grains of garnet.) Minerals such as ilmenite and magnetite, an iron ore, are plentiful on some beaches, such as Block Island's (Rhode Island) Crescent Beach, which was mined in colonial times for material to blot manuscript ink and which often fools tourists today into thinking, from its black appearance, that a recent oil spill has soiled the shore.

Thus, each seashore is, in essence, a wonderous natural craft store filled with interesting, challenging, and stimulating raw materials with which to exercise your natural creativity. And yet what these wild edges offer you today is little different from what they offered to your ancesters many years ago.

Mankind's fascination with the sea and its treasures began with a passion thousands and thousands of years ago. Settlers in central France treasured **seashells** as jewlery, Virgil and other Romans collected shells as a hobby, and a seashell collection was even found in the ruins of Pompeii. Countless people

Surf clam

around the world, both past and present, have discovered the potential of sea treasures, including the Duchess of Richmond and her two daughters, who started work on the Shell Pavilion at Goodwood Park, Sussex, in 1739. Completed after many years, it stands today as a lasting tribute to wild-edge creativity—and, as well, to perseverance.

In America, the Native Americans were the first to discover the many delicacies and delights provided by the ocean, including the pleasure of summer months spent at the seashore. Many northeastern tribes who wintered inland migrated to the bays and Atlantic coastal areas as soon as the weather warmed, seeking the abundance of foods from the sea and salt marshes. The earliest migration was for the April fishing season when shad, a variety of saltwater fish related to the herring but with a meatier body, was caught and then baked with wild leeks, sunflower seeds, and sunflower-seed butter. Later on, bluefish, scrod, cod, oysters, clams, mussels, halibut, scallops, and seaweeds such as dulce, kelp, and **Irish moss** were harvested from the sea and the shore. Accompanied by great feasting and ceremonial celebrations, these summer seaside periods offered a welcome change from the Indians' woodland diet.

Time spent near the ocean was also time for Indians to seek and amass their fortunes from the lowly mollusk known as the quahog. The name *Mercenaria mercenaria* was given to the northern quahog by Carl Linnaeus (the man who created the binomial system for naming plants and animals) because of the Indians' use of its shell to make wampum beads, a common medium of exchange within and among the various Indian tribes. Although wampum, or the cylindrical fragments made from the shell, was also made from whelk and periwinkle shells, purple beads from quahog shells had twice the value of white whelk and periwinkle wampum. The Indians displayed their wealth like jewlery, in personal adornments; strings of wampum beads, arranged in patterns by color, were worn as necklaces or woven together into belts and headbands.

The early colonists also valued what they could harvest from the sea and the shore, for a variety of reasons. Around the house, they used scallop shells as individual baking dishes, skimmed the fat from soups or the cream from milk with large flat clamshells, and ate their cornmeal mush with clamshell spoons. Women and children often journeyed to the seaside to collect the plentiful and beautiful seashells, which they then arranged in a row on a shelf, heaped in a basket near a window or on a table, or used as pin trays or flower containers. Colonial women began a shell art form that has been copied ever since, in which small shells were glued to paper or wood in patterns that resembled mosaics or shell flowers; in the Victorian period in America, such simple shell flowers grew into elaborately constructed pyramids, which were displayed on mantels, niches, and tables.

Colonial men went to the sea as fishermen and whalers. Fish was so valued that, in the 1600s, the Massachusetts Bay Colony banned the use of the striped bass as well as cod for fertilizer because they were deemed too good for such a purpose. And New England farmers indirectly interacted with the wild edges by building nesting platforms to attract the osprey because mated osprey pairs were extremely territorial and would defend their entire neighborhood, including the farmers' chicken yards, from hawks and other chicken-stealing raptors.

❧

There was a time when wild, pristine coastline dotted the Atlantic seaboard and you could walk great lengths of the Atlantic shore freely. (In *Cape Cod*, for example, Henry David Thoreau wrote that he walked the length of the Cape Cod beaches more than once, taking his time and taking advantage of lodging with local folks and lighthouse keepers.) Nowadays, however, few lighthouses remain—those that do, warn the public to stay away—and the coast has become increasingly restricted, largely as a result of protective private interests. More and more stretches of coastline are now inaccessible by virtue of having become built on, fenced, or surrounded by private property.

However, the National Park Service, U.S. Fish and Wildlife service, and various state and local agencies have kept large stretches of beach open to all. There are guidelines that need to be followed whenever you venture out onto these wild edges on your natural creativity expeditions. These guidelines are designed to protect endangered species as well as dunes and, too, to keep you out of danger.

Islands and beaches survive because of plants. Vegetation such as beach grass, wild rose, poverty grass, seaside goldenrod, and wide-leafed beach pea is oftentimes the only barrier to the dynamic beach air—even a breeze as gentle as nine miles per hour can pick up sand and blow it away. "The relationship between vegetation and beaches is like some good marriages," observes Philip Kopper in his book *The Wild Edge: Life and Lore of the Great Atlantic Beaches*, "slowly productive, fundamentally stable through small accommodations by each party and occasionally but not fatally tumultuous. To overstate for the example's sake: An established island fails when things get too rough for the ever-accepting plants or when the vegetation doesn't hold up its end of the bargain and lets things fall apart."

Inner dune

Beach vegetation plays a vital role in the life of the shores and salt marshes, trapping grains of sand that would otherwise roll past, attracting insects that are eaten by the birds that nest in the protective cover provided by the hardy plants, and anchoring both the plant and the materials it grows in with its roots. Because of this, collecting even one sample of beach plant can be disruptive to the entire beach. So, sketch or photograph vegetation, but do not take even the tiniest sample.

As uncomfortable as it may be, wear shoes while beachcombing, and don protective gloves. Used hypodermic needles, medical waste, broken glass, and other waste products may, unfortunately, be part of the "buried treasures" you inadvertently step on or dig up in your natural-creativity explorations on the wild edge. Too, surface sand can get hot enough in the sun to blister bare feet; rocks and shells can inflict nasty wounds; algae-covered breakwater rocks can be slippery. As well, wear protective sunscreen and/or a hat and other clothing to guard against sunburn.

As you explore all areas of a beach, including the tidal pools, breakwater rocks, and sandbars for interesting shells and the like, remember that the seaside is a living habitat. Shells are not always empty and sea creatures that may look or act like they are dead may be very much alive; taking them away from their home will surely kill them. *Never* remove an occupied seashell, live starfish or urchin, or any other living thing; *never* attempt to pull or scrape a shell from a rock or other interesting collectible to which it is clinging. Collect only empty shells or specimens that are clearly dead.

Be aware of where you are going and, as well, the time of tidal changes. A place that you can easily reach with dry shoes in the morning can be the same place you are later stranded on by the frigid waters of high tide. Some places are islands at high tide and peninsulas at low. *Pay attention!* Time passes quickly when you get caught up in the pleasurable experience of beachcombing. Too, keep in mind that all written tidal information is *approximate*—so allow yourself a broad margin of safety.

Finally, although you may be sorely tempted, never beachcomb during inclement weather. Even a "weak" hurricane—classified as a Category 1—boasts a mean wind speed of 74 to 95 miles per hour with a storm surge height of four to five feet. And a thunder-and-lightening storm on the beach—which can be quite dramatic—is actually quite dangerous considering the close proximity of water and the fact that you may be the tallest local object that could be struck by lightning. If you are caught in a sudden lightning storm, crouch down behind a dune—not an isolated tree, bush, or wood or metal watchtower, which may draw a bolt to it like a magnet. The National Oceanic and Atmospheric Administration instructions state that if "you feel your hair stand on end—indicating that lightning is about to strike—drop on your knees and bend forward, putting your hands on your knees. Do not lie flat on the ground."

❧

With these safety precautions in mind, exercising your wild-edge natural creativity involves two completely different—but equally pleasurable—experiences. One is beachcombing, or collecting what interests you from your strolls along the seashore in order to create interesting objects and displays. The other is saltwater harvesting in order to enjoy the "delicacies de la mer"—the delicacies of the sea—on your dinner table.

BEACHCOMBING

Beachcombing is, to many, an art form which, in reality, has little form. As Pamela Westland urges in her book *The Step by Step Art of Nature Crafts*: "Comb the beaches for shells and sea lavender, dried seaweed and scraps of discarded rope. Look for decorative materials that may be craggy and rugged or pearly and elegant, to recapture the tantalizing tang of the sea." In other words, as long as something comes from the sea, collect it. You will eventually find a creative use for it, even if it means that you just place it in a basket tray along with other gifts from the sea.

There may be a time of day that is best to collect seaside wares, such as the early morning hours, or a time of year known for its generous array of seaside treasures, such as the winter months, when storms and unsettled weather churn the sea and there is less competition from fair-weather beachcombers. But no matter what time of day or what season, any and every walk on the beach can be a treasure hunt: polished stones, colorful shells and bits of shells, sandworn beach glass, sea stars, sand dollars, hardened starfish, bits of coral, sea urchins, crab shells and claws, dried sponges and seaweed, floats and nets, and driftwood. All of these—and many other seashore finds—can be used in a multitude of creations.

So, whenever you journey to the beach, carry plastic storage bags, shopping bags, empty containers, or a basket in which to hold the treasures as you collect them. Then, when you arrive home, sort through your treasures. Brush them off and/or wash and rinse them in warm, soapy water. Sea snails (**one-shell homes**) may require some extra rinsing and shaking out of sand, which may lodge far inside the spiral. Set the wet treasures out on sheets of newspaper to dry,

Common periwinkle then store in labeled boxes or plastic storage bags until ready to use.

The best way to create and then display your seaside collectibles is to use them "as is." Scraping barnacles from shells, repairing a frayed piece of netting, or spraying or rubbing oil or shellac on seashells detracts from their true appearance. In fact, even broken bits of shells can make dramatic displays or be used creatively in your crafts.

Sometimes the most intriguing displays are those in which bigger shells are used as holders for smaller shells and bits of shells, dried chunks of seaweed, and smooth stones. Dried seaweed can be placed in baskets with your dried weeds and grasses for wall displays, in wreaths to add interesting color and texture, or painted with gay colors and then hung from driftwood "trees" as ornaments. Seashells can serve as candle holders in any room, as place-card holders in the dining room, or as a dish for bath-oil beads in the bathroom. Glass preserving jars can be effective storage containers for shells and beach glass, as well as shell display cases when placed in front of a window or accent light. Shells can be glued to an ordinary plastic plant pot or container to create an attractive container in which to display dried weeds, a plant, kitchen utensils, pencils and pens, and so on. Shells can be glued or sewn onto a straw sunhat to make a beachcombers hat; used to embellish picture or mirror frames; made into necklaces and earrings transformed into Christmas-tree decorations, or used as part of the decorative wrapping for a gift.

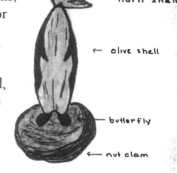

← horn shell

← olive shell

← butterfly

← nut clam

Shell creature: Penguin

You can also make decorative creations solely out of shells. For example, a **penguin** could be made out of a horn shell, olive shell, butterfly shell, and nut clam shell, with wings painted on with black enamel. Animal sculptures, flowers, or other intriguing shell creations can be built out of a combination of shells, beach pebbles, and other seaside treasures as well as raw materials previously gathered on your forays into other nature locales.

SALTWATER HARVESTING

Your ancestors learned long ago that the sea is where seafood lives. Today you can replicate this ancestral saltwater harvesting by catching, netting, digging, or trapping your own fish and shellfish— and then preparing what you harvest in a tasty dish or as a meal all by itself. (Of course, you never have to go home empty-handed from a harvest or if you are a bit squeamish about handling fresh-caught sea creatures; simply buy the seafood fresh from a dockside market or a skipper on the dock.)

No license is necessary to catch fish from the sea; in fact, many national seashores allow you to take a "reasonable amount" of shellfish "for personal use," although some require permits and each locale may differ in its regulations. Know what is acceptable before you venture out on your harvests. From time to time, clam beds may be closed for public-health reasons. Clams are filter feeders, which means they strain the water to filter out their microscopic food, thus retaining and concentrating toxic substances from tainted water in their systems. The dreaded "red tide," an unexplained population explosion of certain plankton that renders fin and shellfish fatally poisonous for brief periods, also will shut down saltwater harvesting.

But after you familiarize yourself with local regulations and are assured there are no health warnings, harvest away! Cast your rod and reel from the shoreline or fish in the marsh with a baited string and see what you can hook. Hunt for quahogs and cherrystone clams at low tide in mud or sand on sandbars, in the protected waters of bays, and in tide-fed pools. Use your fingers or a clam shell to dig; be sure to carry a bucket filled with sea water to keep what you harvest fresh until you arrive home. **Softshell clams** require a bit more work

Long-necked clam

because of their twelve-inch siphons, or breathing tubes, which allow them to burrow deep in dense mud. Clam rakes can be used to dig around the air holes. After you arrive home with your softshell-clam harvest, store the clams in a bucket of cool fresh water for a while before cooking. Clams taken from soft mud need anywhere from an hour to a couple of days to flush their systems of internal sand, which gives the clams a gritty texture when eaten. Blue mussels cling to rocks and pilings in active, wave-washed places and can best be pried from these sites during low tide. Softshell crabs can be taken by net alone (be careful: they *will* pinch) from their hiding places in the shallow fringes of a bay or, if you are particularly adventureous, you can tie a chicken neck to a length of string, toss the neck into shallow water, and stay still for a few minutes. Then, every few minutes or so, give the string a gentle tug to see if it meets with the resistance of a nibbling crab or one that is trying to walk away with the bait. Pull the string up slowly, then quickly snatch a net underneath the crab below the bait; the crab will let go if it senses movement.

Most other ocean fish, including fin fish, are best obtained during a deep-sea fishing expedition, which provides a boat, the equipment, and a crew skilled in finding the best fishing grounds. Oftentimes such operations will also clean, gut, scale, and cut steaks and fillets from what you catch, thereby limiting your preparation of the fish to seasoning and cooking—and, of course, enjoying what you have harvested from the sea!

ANCESTRAL NATURAL CREATIVITY CHALLENGE:

U'NEGA'GEI—IROQUOIS SOUP

This is a tasty soup that is both light enough for summer fare and hearty enough for cold winter nights. To make this soup you will need

> *2–3-pound fish (haddock, scrod, or cod) cleaned*
>   *but with the skin and bones*
> *3 quarts of water*
> *1 large onion, diced*
> *2 cups dried lima beans*
> *2 tablespoons fine yellow or white cornmeal*
> *2 tablespoons chopped fresh parsley*
> *1 teaspoon chopped fresh or dried basil*
> *1 teaspoon chopped fresh or dried dillweed*
> *1 clove garlic*

Place the fish in a large pot or kettle and simmer, uncovered, for thirty minutes. Carefully lift out the fish. Remove the skin and bones. Flake or cut the fish into chunks, then return to the water. Add the rest of the ingredients. Simmer for about an hour, or until the beans are soft. Serve steaming hot. The soup improves with time; freeze leftover soup or store in the refrigerator for up to a week.

————————————————————————————————

What you can find at the wild edges of nature can be astounding. In the three decades that *The Wild Edge* author Philip Kopper has been beachcombing, he has found

> . . . two nearly complete whale skeletons, a recently deceased porpoise with lovely pearly teeth, a Chevrolet, three loggerhead turtles, enough bleach bottles to launder the Sixth Fleet and enough assorted barrels to fill a delicatessen, one rusty tricycle, a perambulator, many gloves and boots (always filled with sand), an 18-foot sailboat with her back broken, an almost whole pilot whale that couldn't be approached downwind without a gas mask, one 16-foot runabout with an outboard motor, uncounted pieces of wooden hulls and decks, a barge large enough to carry six freight cars, a hundredweight of antique iron ships' nails in worm-eaten timbers, a yard of oyster-encrusted cable that looked like a sea snake, one half-full squeeze bottle of Spanish pomade, innumerable bottles (never with a note), several fishnet floats, a gill net with about a hundred pounds of spoiled fish, three jet-fuel tanks, one anchor and chain, miles of hawsers, two willing girls, half a catamaran, and one loving couple.

While shells will probably be the most sensible things you can collect on your seaside natural creativity explorations, always leave yourself open to new possibilities. The wild edges are filled with their own wild and wonderful surprises!

Exercising Your Seaside Natural Creativity

1. See if you can find compass grass, so named for the circles its bending leaves make in sand on a windy day, which inhibits sand movement in any direction. Observe the wind-generated motions and habitats of other seaside vegetation; give each a name that fits its actions, appearance, or other distinguishing features. Compile a

sketchbook of some of these grasses, flowering plants, shrubs, and trees.

2. Collect the shed shells—or exoskeletons—of crabs such as horseshoe crabs, Atlantic blue crabs, "king" crabs, rock crabs, green crabs, and so on from the beach or bring home a "doggy bag" of the claws and body shells left over from a crab or lobster dinner. Soak the shells overnight in mild, soapy water to loosen soft tissue or meat from the body armor. Let the shells dry. Then experiment with painting on these shells—create an ocean scene, for instance, or "restore" the shells to their original color to give them a life-like appearance. You can then use the painted shells as part of a beach centerpiece or other display of seaside treasures.

3. All seashells come from one great big family called Mollusca, or Mollusks, which comprises thousands and thousands of members. Entire field guides are devoted to seashells that can be found in a particular region of the country. Basically, however, there are two types of seashells: the clam and the snail. Clam types are flat or dish-like; snail types are usually spiral or cone-shaped. Beyond those two distinctions, shells are often named for the way they look—the tulip, the olive, the slipper, and so on.

As you beachcomb, collect shells with interesting shapes. Try to determine, from the shape of each shell, what the name of the shell is. Then use a field guide to find out how close you were to guessing the name of the shell. Create your own visual identification chart of shell samples and names for future reference.

4. Hold a sand castle–building contest with your friends or family members. Allow only beach treasures to be used in the creation of each castle. Award prizes in a variety of categories, such as Most Beautifully Landscaped, Craziest Design, Dreamiest Castle, and so on. Take a picture of the finished castles, then keep them in a *Sand Castle Beautiful* scrapbook.

5. Take a large pad of thick drawing paper, glue, and paints or crayons to the beach. Create an abstract sand painting by squirting glue arbitrarily over a sheet of paper and then sprinkling sand onto the wet glue. Allow the glue to dry, then tilt the paper so the extra sand falls off the page. You can embellish your abstract sand print with seashells and other beach treasures. Or you can first sketch a design on paper that creatively employs sand. Spread the glue where

the picture requires the sand, then sprinkle the sand onto the wet glue. Add details and color to the painting with watercolors, marking pens, or crayons.

6. Make seashell chimes out of a driftwood branch, yarn or string, and seashells of various sizes and shapes. Look for shells that already have a hole through them so the holes through which the yarn or string will pass will not have to be drilled.

7. Use a clamshell to make a tiny cactus garden. Buy the smallest variety of cactus available from a flower shop; some reach only an inch high when fully grown. Place a drop of white glue inside the shell and set the cactus on it. Then combine sand with fine pebbles to fill in around the cactus. Place in a sunny location, and water once a week.

8. Some bivalve shells, when open but still hinged, resemble an insect's wings in shape and, sometimes, in color. While beachcombing, if you find a hinged bivalve, safeguard it from breaking apart. Later on, glue the hinged shell or shells to a long, slender univalve shell to create a butterfly or dragonfly. Use twigs or dried grass for antennae. Then display the insect on a log or other natural habitat. (You can also make a mobile to display several insects made in this way.)

9. Become familiar with the flavor of cod, a fish that is often associated with New England's best-known Cape but is abundant year-round in coastal waters. Cod was a mainstay in the diets of both the Indians and the colonists, who would boil the head and shoulders of the fish and then slice and fry or broil the remaining fish. Scrod is simply young cod, no more than two pounds in size, and is usually broiled. To make broiled scrod, place a piece of fish in a greased pan. Sprinkle with sunflower seed oil and season with pepper, dillweed, and parsley. The Indians served this fish hot, accompanied by wild greens and cranberries.

10. Go on a deep-sea fishing expedition. Head out on a whale watch. Spend the day island-hopping in a nearby bay. Have lunch in a seacoast village. Visit a maritime museum. Do any or all of these things to stimulate your wild-edge natural creativity.

7

WILD WATER: *Natural Creativity from Wetland, Stream, and Sky*

Never in his life had he seen a river before—this sleek, sinuous, full-bodied animal, chasing and chuckling, gripping things with a gurgle and leaving them with a laugh, to fling itself on fresh playmates that shook themselves free, and were caught and held again....tired at last, he sat on the bank, while the river still chattered on to him, a babbling procession of the best stories in the world, sent from the heart of the earth to be told at last to the insatiable sea. — English writer KENNETH GRAHAME

We get a little snow, then a few inches, then another inch or two, and sometimes we get a ton. The official snow gauge is a Sherwin-Williams paint can stuck to the table behind the town garage, with the famous Sherwin-Williams globe and red paint spilling over the Arctic icecap. When snow is up to the top of the world, then there is a ton of snow.

— American humorist GARRISON KEILLOR

EARTH'S ABUNDANCE OF WATER in the form of rivers, lakes, and oceans has earned her the nickname—Blue Planet. Earth's water is the ultimate setting for life. All life began with water, as evidenced by fossils that show that the first animals were aquatic; too, all life continues to be supported by water, as evidenced by the vegetation and animal life so prevalent around lakes, rivers, streams, wetlands, and even the tiniest pools of water.

WILD WATER OF WETLANDS

It is because of the increasing awareness of the integral value water has in supporting and sustaining life on Earth that the wild water of wetlands has become such a hot political issue. The planet is still reeling from the draining and filling in of large tracts of wetlands that have occurred since the beginning of European settlement—a total of sixty-five million acres to date—due in large part to the misunderstood role the wetlands have had in sustaining and supporting life. Currently, unless another wetland is created to replace it, an existing wetland has legal protection from being filled in.

Such marshy areas—once called swamps and looked at disdainfully by casual observers as being odorous, bug-infested, useless parts of the planet—are magnets to naturalists as well as to nature, for the shallow bodies of still water welcome plant growth both in and surrounding the water, creating all sorts of protective nooks and crannies for nesting animals. Too, wetlands stunningly showcase the interconnectedness of nature, where insect eggs hatch into nymphs before sprouting wings and flying away; where tadpoles hatch from a string of eggs and then transform into toads that hop along the forest floor; and where ducks, geese, and shorebirds nest safely. Wetlands are also vital to mankind's survival: like sponges, they soak up heavy rainfall and thus reduce flooding; they capture and neutralize surface pollutants and thus help purify the ground water for drinking; and they are breeding grounds for a wide variety of essential wildlife, thus assisting in the comeback of many species of duck that have been impacted by the loss of wetlands.

Perhaps the most dominant wildlife in any wetland—and, as well, the best advertisement for the location of a wetland—is the cattail. The **cattail** proliferates because of the countless seeds it scatters at the end of every growing season via an explosion of cloudy seeds and fluff, as well as the rootlike structures (called rhizomes) that it sends up under the thick muck.

The cattail is a plant of many uses. When picked at maturity and dried thoroughly, its thick brown top and

sturdy stem make it the perfect addition to a dried everlasting decoration or dramatic when displayed alone. (Be sure to lightly spray the
brown tops of cattails with shellac or hair spray after collecting in
order to seal in the fluff; otherwise, as it dries, the top will open and
cattail fuzz will end up all over everything!) Fresh stems can be
picked early in the growing season and then trained into graceful
curves while drying, adding a more distinctive appearance to a dried
arrangement. Or the thick stems
can be picked at full maturity, dried,
and then sliced with a razor to size
and used like bamboo to create a
cattail serving tray, cup or glass
holder, planter, and so on.

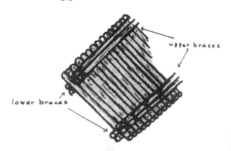

Cattail serving tray

In the early spring, as the cattails are sprouting upward and
before the flower stalks emerge,
cattail stalks can be pulled upward
by grasping the center of the plant and then the stalks peeled away
to remove the white, syrupy core. This soft white center can be eaten
raw, sliced like onions into a salad, or cooked like any other vegetable. In fact, steamed cattail stems (also known as cossack asparagus) was once a common vegetable of the Native Americans, who
served the boiled, tender stalks with nut oil and cider vinegar dressing. The roots, which are rich in starch, can be eaten like potatoes.
And the clear, syrupy juice from this marshland vegetable functions,
like today's cornstarch, as a natural thickener when added to soups,
stews, or other vegetable broths.

Cattail fluff, or down, which spreads the seeds of
future generations of plants, has been used in jackets,
baseballs, and mattresses. The pollen, known to be
highly flammable, served as tinder in a pinch. Large
quantities of leaves were gathered, dried, and then
used by Native Americans to make bas-
kets and by settlers to make rush seats for
their chairs. Even leftover dried catttail
leaves were put to good use by America's
early ancestors in the creation of a variety
of children's playthings, including a **cattail duck** and a cattail doll.

ANCESTRAL NATURAL CREATIVITY CHALLENGE:

CATTAIL DOLL

You can make your own cattail doll (see illustration in the Introduction) out of dried cattail leaves. After midsummer—but before frost arrives in your area—collect green cattail leaves when they are at their fullest height. Cut individual leaves above the root crown. (If you choose to cut the stalks for use in other natural creativity projects, detach the leaves from the stalks as soon as possible; they need good circulation to combat mold.) Stand the leaves on the floor with the thicker ends down; do not stack. Dry thoroughly before use in a shady spot in order to preserve the delicate green color. Each stalk will shrink to two thirds of its width during this drying process.

When the leaves have dried, split them down the center; thinner strips will make it easier to shape the head of the doll. Soak the leaves for an hour or so in water, until pliable. Then cut the leaves to a length twice as long as the doll. Bend each leaf in half without creasing. Place the strips side to side as well as front to back as you form the doll. Tie off the neck with a thin cattail strip when the head is well rounded. Bend and insert a short piece of cattail stalk for the arms. Finally, tie off the waist to secure the arms.

Some of the most beautiful and watertight baskets were made centuries ago by American Indians from fibrous plants and grasses that grew in or near fresh water. Such natural-basketry marsh plants, which include species of rushes, sedges, and reed grass (as well as cattail leaves) can be found today growing in the shallows of wetlands as well as in roadside and suburban development ditches, near watershed and dam projects, and alongside lakes and rivers. (To distinguish between these sometimes confusing members of the grasslike families, use the adage "**Sedges** have edges and rushes are round.") After picking, all plants air-dry easily. When picked at different stages of their maturity, sedges will dry silvery gray, gold, or deep brown.

Sedges

Native American basket makers, both past and present, believe that natural basketry roots them to the earth and, as well, helps them to seek the council of the plant kingdom, which, according to Indian legend, is humanity's helper. Long ago, as the legend goes, the animals came together in their tribal councils and complained that humanity was no longer showing them respect or consideration, killing them not out of need but out of sport or fear. The animals decided to teach the "two-leggeds" a lesson for this treatment, giving them illnesses and diseases. The plants, however, had no such complaints against humans. So they decided, by council vote, to help the "two-leggeds" overcome the illnesses and diseases brought on them by the animals, for the plants knew that all things must remain in balance.

Today, gathering plants from wetlands, carefully drying and then rewetting the stems and leaves to restore suppleness, and patiently refining the skills necessary to create with them allows you not just the opportunity for establishing or reestablishing a close contact with the natural world but helps to relieve stress, thereby making wild water-plant life a most valuable medicine for combatting illness and disease.

Collecting rushes, sedges, and cattails from wetlands and other still-water locales is reasonably safe, but be aware of possible dangers presented by poisonous plants (such as poison ivy), injurious underbrush (such as pricker bushes), and unwelcome living things (such as stinging insects or snakes). Learn to recognize poisonous plants that grow in your area. Wear gloves, long pants, and long sleeves. Take along insect repellent; a netted hat is a good deterrent when bugs are really bad. (Check your clothing and skin when you leave the collecting area; take a thorough shower and launder your clothes when you arrive home.) Make noise while collecting to alert wildlife to your presence. Snakes and other aquatic critters tend to avoid confrontation with humans; trouble comes only when they feel threatened or cornered.

Wear waterproof boots to keep your feet dry. Cut plants rather than pull them out by the roots to ensure next year's growth. Take only what you need. Respect the privacy of nesting waterfowl.

WILD WATER OF RIVERS AND STREAMS

Whereas wetlands are areas in which the water is not moving, is not too deep, and creates a foundation of abundant and easily seen plant and animal life, the wild water of rivers and streams is completely different. Animal tracks on banks oftentimes reveal the proximity of animals, but not their presence, and, although a river or stream may wind through a lush forest or thicket, the faster the rate of water movement, the less plant life it can actually sustain.

But what free-flowing water does offer for exploring your natural creativity are rocks of all shapes, sizes, and colors that have been made round and smooth by the constant rushing waters. These rocks can take on a gemlike appearance or an interesting shape that can be displayed as is; they can be combined with other rocks to create a rock animal or even a much larger structure such as a stone wall; or they can be used in replicating one of the most primitive of all forms of natural creativity—rock art, or stone painting.

Stone painting is the perfect melding of natural ancestral creativity with modern crafting supplies. Early man's primitive cave sketches, with their muted earth tones and crude interpretations, have evolved—with the help of today's tough, inexpensive acrylic paints and finishes—into rock art that brings the stones to life with vibrant colors and a lifelike appearance. Artist Lin Wellford, author of *The Art of Painting Animals on Rocks*, tells of her own accidental—and quite pleasant—experience of stumbling upon rock art:

> Shortly after moving to the Ozark Mountains of northwest Arkansas, I picked up a stone the size and shape of a baking potato at a local creek. It looked so much like a rabbit that I felt moved to take it home and give it eyes, ears and a fluffy cotton tail. From the moment I placed tiny white sparkles in the eyes, I was hooked. The transformation from a dull creek rock into a wild rabbit, one that actually seemed to be looking back at me, was almost magical.

Over the past fifteen years I have painted thousands of stone animals. My menagerie has expanded to include creatures as diverse as reptiles, birds and practically anything with a fur coat.

Although rocks are, in fact, so common and plentiful that few would consider them to have any value, collecting stones on which to paint even a simple drawing can turn into an enjoyable and rewarding treasure hunt. The less pitted the surface of the rock is, the easier it will be to paint; the more interesting the shape of the rock, the more creative you can be in what you make of it. Because of this, rocks that have been tumbled and smoothed by water are often the best. Roadside creeks and streams are ideal places to gather such stones. If you are unsure of where to find such free-flowing waters in your area, talk to someone who fishes or hunts.

Whether the stones are found close to home or while out on a vacation, such rocks are valued souvenirs—pleasant reminders of places visited—as well as carefully chosen candidates for craft projects. A certain amount of time and energy needs to be put into rock gathering. While at first you may not know exactly what you are looking for, certain shapes, textures, and sizes may strike your fancy or even persuade you to see a finished product: a lump may suggest a resting animal's head; a crease or superficial crack a tail or a space between two nesting animals; a protrusion a rocky cliff for a seaside coastal scene.

Look for rocks that have at least one relatively flat side that will prevent it from wobbling or falling over after you finish your painting. Unless you are building a critter out of more than one stone, select stones that are at least a couple of inches thick in order to enhance the details of your painting as well as give you enough room on which to paint. Small, smooth, flat stones, however, are ideal for making Native American spirit stones, or stones on which a picto-graph is painted as a **totem**, or power symbol for personal connection to the essence of the living creature repre-sented by the totem. Totems include

Totem power stones

animal tracks as well as outlines of insects, reptiles, amphibians, birds, and mammals.

Before you begin painting, thoroughly clean the rocks you have collected. Use scouring powder and a scrub brush to remove caked-on algae; warm, soapy water to get rid of loose debris; or a simple sprayer with a garden hose or kitchen sink sprayer to wash away dust. Towel dry the rocks or let them dry outdoors in the sun before painting.

You may use chalk or a pencil to sketch an outline on the rock prior to painting. Because rocks are three-dimensional, plan out all "views" of your painting—front, both sides, and back. Then use the wide variety of acrylic paints available and brushes of varying sizes to paint your totem, critter, or scene. To protect your rock painting once the paint is dry and to make the colors look even brighter, dry seal the surface with a spray-on polyurethane or wipe-on acrylic finish such as a clear floor polish. Display your finished rock art indoors or, for a startling effect or conversation piece, place it outdoors, in its natural habitat; position an owl on a dead tree stump, for instance, or nestle a rabbit in your herb bed.

WILD WATER FROM THE SKY

Wild water from the sky—or, more specifically, snow—is one of the more exciting natural raw materials to work with, because, if you are fortunate enough to live in an area that experiences snowy winters, it drops right at your feet. Step outside your door, and there it is: millions of exquisite crystals—each one different—all packed tightly together, just waiting to be shaped and formed into whatever your imagination seeks to create. Become a child again, and form and throw snowballs. Make a snow fort. Carve out a snow tunnel. Construct an igloo. Build a snowman—or snow woman, snow family, snow dog, or snow anything. Or stack up big snowballs just as you would to make an old-fashioned snowman, except make the pillar of snow as high as possible without it becoming wobbly or tippy. Then use a heavy kitchen knife or hunting knife to carve out a **snow totem pole**, with animals and birds stacked one on top of the other and the traditional thunderbird as the crest at the top of the totem pole. Use food coloring or natural dyes to add color. Then aim a spotlight at the finished totem pole for a dramatic nighttime display, or carve out holes at various places in the pole in which to place lit candles.

Although the time frame in which you can take advantage of a sufficient dumping of this natural raw material may be minimal and, as well, the time in which you have to display your finished product outdoors may be short—one hour of bright sunshine can transform the most intricately worked snow sculpture into a pile of unrecognizable

Snow totem pole

slush—snow creating can be one of the more pleasurable and rewarding ways of spending time outdoors in the winter.

You can also bring the snow indoors and put it to some very tasty uses. Heat maple syrup to boiling, then immediately pour onto clean, white snow to create maple candy. Or make an ancestral version of vanilla ice cream by mixing handfuls of snow with one teaspoon of vanilla, one cup of sugar (or other sweetener), and one can of condensed milk until the mixture looks and tastes like ice cream. You can also add fresh berries, canned fruits, chocolate chips, or flavorings to make other ice cream varieties.

❧

So the next time cattails advertise the location of a wetland or you spot a stream meandering along the side of the road, stop and treat yourself to the sights, smells, sounds, and natural creativity treasures that can be found in such wild-water places. And the next time that rain and snow fall freely upon you, think of ways of tinkering with such things so you can exercise not just your back, shoulder, or arm muscles, but, as well, your creative muscles.

Exercising Your Natural Creativity with Wild Water

1. Find out where the nearest wetland is, then visit it. Pick a good vantage spot, then quietly observe the comings and goings of wetland wildlife. Take along a sketchbook or camera to record your

observations. Then return several times throughout the year to note any changes in plant growth, water level, aquatic life, and so on.

2. Collect a variety of rushes, sedges, and cattails. Allow them to dry. Note their differences in appearance. Then experiment with each plant's qualities by using each in a simple braiding or weaving process. Note the plant's texture, pliability, strength, durability, and so on. Combine two or more plants together to create a simple woven mat.

3. Colors were very important to the American Indians and were widely used in their natural basketry creations. Red signified divinity and power; blue indicated truth and faith; green, the color of spring, signified hope; yellow or gold was the emblem of the sun and showed warmth and fruitfulness; white stood for purity and peace. Soak cattail leaves, rushes, or sedges in coffee, tea, crushed-berry juice, or another natural dye prior to use in order to add a unique appearance to your natural creativity projects.

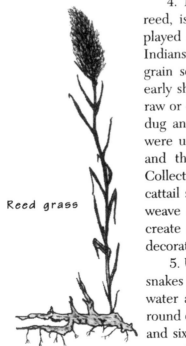

Reed grass

4. **Reed grass**, also known as the common reed, is one of the tallest marsh plants. It once played a vital role in the lives of the American Indians as well as the colonists. The seeds were a grain source for gruels, cereals, and breads; the early shoots were a vegetable that could be eaten raw or cooked; the sweet roots and rhizomes were dug and roasted year-round; and the long stems were used to make arrow shafts and for weaving and thatching. Locate reed grass in a marsh. Collect some of it, and then dry it thoroughly. Use cattail stems to create a spoke arrangement, then weave resoaked reed grass through the spokes to create a mat, a mobile, or an interesting woven decoration to display in a window.

5. Use a guide book to determine what banded snakes are prevalent in your area. Then look in wild water and bring home a "coiled snake stone"—a round or oval rock about two or three inches thick and six or seven inches across. Clean and dry the stone. Sketch the snake's head in the middle of the stone. Then draw the body coils around it so that the tip of the tail

ends up at the bottom of one side of the stone. Use acrylic paints to replicate the colored bands. Place the snake stone in your garden, its natural habitat, for a clever display.

6. Create rock sculptures with more than one rock. To do so, use a rockcraft glue that has the consistency of marshmallow syrup and retains flexibility while working with the stones as well as durability when dry to keep the stones firmly cemented together even while being handled. Decorate your sculpture with paint and/or natural raw materials such as feathers, twigs, and so on.

7. Objects that are naturally found in water, such as shells, beach glass, and tumbled stones, often reveal stronger colors when placed in a water-filled bowl or clear vase. Position this simple but elegant display near a natural or artificial source of light.

8. Appreciate snow by venturing outside during a snowfall with a hand lens and looking at the flakes up close. Wear a plain dark jacket or tape dark construction paper onto one sleeve of your jacket. Study the design of the fresh flakes that fall on your jacket or the paper through a hand lens. Then sketch some of the designs you see or recreate some of the flakes with white paper and scissors.

9. Place a clean pan or bucket outdoors during a rainstorm. Later on, use the collected rainwater to wash your hair. Notice the difference—if any—in washing your hair with rainwater. Is it shinier? Does it feel softer? Is it lighter in color?

10. Gather your friends, neighbors, or family members together and make a communal snow sculpture display. You can create an Indian village, for example, complete with tipis, horses, and a "campfire" (suggested by an outdoor light with a red, orange, or yellow bulb positioned under a pile of sticks). Position a community of forest animals around a living tree in your yard. Or construct a ski jumper racing down an incline before the jump; outfit your jumper with old skis and poles and dress it in warm attire). Then gather indoors to drink hot cocoa and make maple candy.

8

Wild Earth:
Natural Creativity from the Ground

As for the earth, out of it comes bread; but underneath it is turned
up as by fire.
Its stones are the place of sapphires, and it has dust of gold.

—Job 28: 5–6

A rock has being or spirit, although we may not understand it.
—Native American (Pueblo) writer LESLIE MARMON SILKO

ROCKS AND STONES

OF ALL THE NATURAL RAW MATERIALS that lie about—both on
and in the wild earth—just waiting for you to exercise your natural
creativity with them, rocks and stones are by far more plentiful than
any other material. Yet even though all fifty American states have
something to offer every rock hound, most people largely ignore
stones or consider them to be annoying presences in gardens, on
lawns, and on walking paths. What most people fail to recognize,
however, is that they are living each day on a rock. Planet Earth is
one giant rock—a 4.5-billion-year-old rock, to be exact—that circles
the sun, with ancient rock fragments that make up the mountains
you climb, the seawalls you walk, the stone walls that outline your
property, the rocks in your flower garden, and the small skipping
stones that you nonchalantly fling into a lake.

Throughout history, mankind has depended upon rocks for shelter, hunting, preparing food, and defense. In the period of time known as the Stone Age, hunters shaped spear points, knife blades, hide scrapers, and many other useful tools out of stone. Those who lived during the Bronze Age discovered that molten copper—made by heating malachite and other minerals—

Iron ore

could be mixed with tin, forming a substance known as bronze, which was hard enough to use in swords, spears, and armor. In the Iron Age, **iron ore** was mined, melted (or smelted) to obtain its iron, and then shaped into everything from cast-iron pots to knives.

These periods of time long preceded the modern, industrialized age, when most of the mineral resources—or rocks, which are really aggregates of one or more minerals—have been put to significantly more complicated and durable use. (Graphite, for example, which is used to make "lead" pencils, is composed of only carbon, while granite, an ornamental stone, is made up of several different substances, including quartz, feldspar, and mica.) Today rocks are as much a part of your daily life as the air that you breathe. Granite and marble steps lead into the majestic city skyscraper where you work; the skyscraper is made up of metals which were, in turn, once rocks. You drive home on asphalt and cement roadways, which contain rocks. You sit in front of your fireplace, on your stone hearth, inside your aluminum-sided home (aluminum is made from bauxite ore and other minerals). Your home is lit and heated by the uranium and coal that fuels your local electric power plant. Your watch keeps time with the assistance of quartz. Small rocks, in the form of sand, hold your local farmer's soil together so the corn that you place on your dinner table can grow. Even the adornments you wear—on your fingers, around your neck, in your ears—are made from rocks.

But no matter where rocks come from—igneous rock is derived directly from the mantle of the earth, sedimentary rock is made of sediments composed of tiny particles of sand or carbonates, and metamorphic rocks occur when heat and pressure alter either igneous or sedimentary rock—and no matter how significantly and meaningfully the earth's rocks are incorporated into your daily life—

in schools, churches, homes, shopping malls, and other building construction; in sources of fuel and energy; in computers, telephones, faxes, and other communication systems; in trains, trucks, planes, airplanes, automobiles, and other transportation sytems; in playgrounds, athletic fields, and recreation equipment; and in much, much more—rocks and stones, in their purest and simplest forms and with very little alteration, can provide an endless source of inspiration for discovering and exploring your natural creativity.

❧

People of early America first lived in caves or under overhanging rocks and then, later on, used rocks as building materials for more elaborate homes. In early New Mexico, for example, Indian women baked gypsum rocks, pounded them into powder, and made a soupy paste with which to plaster their adobe walls; the resulting yeso dried to an eye-squinting, dazzling white. Early Americans used

Rocks for grinding

rocks to craft weapons, tools, and ornaments. They used **rocks to grind** fruits and seeds. They used rocks to build unmortared stone boundaries that still stand today. They used rocks, in the form of coal, to heat homes and buildings; later on, they used "coal oil," or kerosene, in lamps, lanterns, and stoves.

The early Americans also used rocks to make metals; in fact, nearly a hundred years before America's first lead mine was opened in southeastern Missouri in 1720 (a Virginia mine that opened a few decades later supplied the lead for bullets used in the Revolutionary War), American Indians had already been mining copper around the northern shore of the region now called Michigan, long before French fur traders infiltrated the area in the 1600s. While these Indians sometimes found copper lumps, or nuggets, lying about in stream beds or on beaches, they predominantly located ledges in which the copper could be seen and then built big fires they kept going all day and all night. When the rock became quite hot, the Indians pushed the fires away and immediately poured cold water on the ledges, making the sizzling rock cool so fast that it cracked. The Indian miners then used stone axes to pound the broken ledges into chips. They sorted through these chips carefully, picking out nuggets of copper that could be hammered into knives, hatchets, needles, and ornaments.

This kind of copper mining by the Indians went on in America for quite some time; some of the mines even went as deep as twenty to thirty feet. But then these Indian miners disappeared; future Indians that settled in the Michigan area did not mine copper or make much use of it. Later on, when rocks in the form of gold nuggets encouraged westward expansion, prospectors found enormous deposits of copper ore that were later mined and used in making a variety of items responsible in assisting the coast-to-coast formation and union of the country, including the copper wires that carried telegraph and telephone messages from the eastern colonies to the western settlements.

But while rocks were employed by America's earliest settlers for survival as well as for practical purposes, rock crafting usually fulfilled ritual or ceremonial functions. The rock art of Native Americans, for example, was not ancient graffiti drawn out of pure enjoyment, as a form of self-expression or as an artistic experience for its creator. Rather, rock art was secular, used to document the relationship between the inner and the outer world. Images of the sun, the constellations, animals, plants, clouds, rivers, and mountains illustrated their cultural and spiritual significance to the people. Such art was often located alongside trails or near places of habitation; these "spirit rocks" served as shrines, as places in which a person's relationship with others, the natural world, and the cosmos could be understood, and as healing sites that were visited for the purposes of health, fertility, prosperity, success in hunting and war, and, too, for rites of passage.

Secular rock art included such images and symbols as:

• **hand prints,** regarded by many native people as prayer requests;

• **anthropomorphs,** or designs made to look somewhat human but which represented a deity or spirit in human form;

anthropomorph

• **zoomorphs,** or spirits or deities in the form of animals. Some of the more common zoomorphs include the bear or bear tracks (to the people who hunted the ferocious bear in the northern part of America, the bear symbolized power; to the Zuni, the bear was a healing "medicine"; to the Bear Clan, the bear paw was a sign of the clan, indicating that the clan had traveled to a particular location); snakes, which, because they live close to the earth, were considered to be patrons of the precious water in and on the earth, and thus able to communicate with the sky beings when rain was needed; and mountain sheep, which represented hunting magic because they were wary and difficult to hunt;

zoomorph: bear track

• **the humpback flute player,** also known as Kokopelli, a symbol who, by playing his flute, calls the clouds to make rain and, because he carries seeds and mist in his hump, spreads fertility and abundance;

humpback flute player

• **masks,** which represent dieties and magical beings, the most common of which are the Kachinas, or supernatural beings associated by Hopi Indians with the origin myth and successful corn harvests;

mask pictograph

• **sky-beings**—the sun, the moon, lightning, birds, and clouds—all of which bring rain and abundance to earth; and

sky-being: the sun

• **abstract figures** that symbolize cosmic and natural forces, such as arcs,

abstract figure: rainbow arc

which represent rainbows or halos; zigzags, which represent the water symbols snakes or lightning; and circles, symbols for the sun but also symbols of unity, indicating "all one people."

Drawing on rock is not the only cultural and spiritual Native American art form that uses rock for crafting. The Zuni Indians, for example, often carried small stone fetishes that resembled frogs, which represented life-giving and life-sustaining rain, as good luck charms. You can find a small, smooth stone, keep it warm by carrying in your pocket, and then touch it and rub it for good luck, much as the Zuni did. Or you can paint an image on the stone that symbolizes a quality you wish to attain whenever you touch the stone, such as an eagle to help you achieve vision and insight.

While most rocks that were crafted had to be chiseled, chipped, or cracked, soapstone could actually be carved. Soapstone, a soft "greasy" stone still mined today as talc for all kinds of industrial purposes as well as for health and beauty products, was originally prized as an art material that was used to create body ornaments, fine bowls, elaborate smoking pipes, and beautiful carved figures. The Inuit (Eskimo) was (and still is) particularly adept at carving figures that seem to radiate life energy; in fact, the Inuit's religion taught that everything in nature—the trees, the sea, the sun, the wind, the snow—had a felt inner spirit, called an *innua*. Stones, along with polar bears, had the most powerful innua of all. Because of this, the relationship the Inuit carver had with stones was almost spiritual; oftentimes the crafter would carry a stone around for months before beginning to work with it, in order to understand the stone. Then, using a carving tool of stone or bone, the sculpture would be formed, polished with another stone, and then rubbed with blubber to bring out the color.

The Inuit were also adept at crafting with fieldstones, which they used to make tools, mortars, bowls, amulets to ward off evil, and lamps that were often part of their marriage rituals. The bowl-shaped marriage lamp—made from a rock hollowed at the center and filled with fat pounded from animal tissue, with a moss wick extending from the center to a flat rim along the edge—was traditionally presented by the Eskimo bride to her husband as a symbol of what she hoped to bring to the marriage: stability, strength, warmth, and light.

ANCESTRAL NATURAL CREATIVITY CHALLENGE:

INUIT MARRIAGE LAMP

You can make an Inuit Marriage Lamp to give to a bride-to-be as a wedding gift or to present to your partner as an anniversary gift. Search for a stone that has a nice color and texture and already suggests the shape of a bowl with a center depression. Test your rock for cracks by pouring water over it; water will darken at the crack lines. Also, test the rock for soundness by tapping (not pounding) it with a hammer. Reject any rock that has a dull thud instead of a ring and/or exhibits cracks.

If the trench in the rock is already deep enough—a saucerlike indentation is fine—but not completely smooth, use a file or hard stone to refine any rough edges. If you need to enlarge or deepen the trench, wear protective goggles and use a mallet and chisel, finishing off the trench with a file.

You can then fill the hollow with a candle wick and candle wax or lay a candle wick in the hollow and present the gift with a bottle of scented or unscented lamp oil. An accompanying card can explain the Eskimo Marriage Lamp tradition and how to safely light it.

Because all land today is owned by someone—whether it be a private individual or the government—no rock or stone is really free for the taking. Therefore, the right thing to do, before collecting stones from any locale, is to seek permission from the appropriate individual or owner to carry it away. Even if you are in a relatively remote locale, it is still a good idea to leave the rocks alone until you can find out who owns the land and/or what the accepted policy is on collecting.

There are several ways to determine where to look for rocks and stones in your area, especially if you are looking for a particular type of stone. The Department of the Interior (Bureau of Mines, Washington, DC 20240) publishes a list of state geologists. From this list, you can then locate and write a letter to a local geologist explaining what your needs are. You will most likely be furnished with a reply that includes information about deposits or mines in the area you wish to explore. Some regional geological highway maps of the American Association of Petroleum Geologists provide a list of selected mineral-, rock-, and fossil-collecting localities and places of geological interest in your region (write to AAPG Bookstore, P.O. Box 979, Tulsa, OK 74101-0979, or call 1-800-364-2274). Museums are also likely sources of information that can help you with a successful rock roundup, as well as rock and mineral clubs, tourist bureaus, and local chambers of commerce.

Quarries, construction sites, and mines are excellent sources of a number of varities of rocks, and more often than not those in charge readily give permission to carry away a few samples or even larger quantities of rocks and stones. Ask the best time for you to do your rock collecting; the construction foreperson will usually encourage collection on Saturday afternoons and Sundays, when work is suspended. (If you can, pay a visit after hard rains, when the water washes out hidden rocks.)

When on site, follow all safety rules. Stay away from unstable edges or areas in which there are visible holes around the rocks, which may indicate a much larger hole underneath. Search the bottoms of cliffs and quarries, where rocks are prevalent and the footing is safe. Never swim in a quarry, even on the hottest collecting day. And, because you will most likely be in a remote area, take along a friend for company as well as for safety in case either of you becomes hurt.

Avoid taking rocks from areas in which the stability of the soil will be compromised if the rocks are removed. Take no rocks that indicate or form paths or that provide barriers along hiking trails. If, on lifting a rock, you discover several "tenants" underneath, gently return the rock to its original position and hunt for other rocks that will create less of an impact, when removed, on those creatures that depend on the rocks for safety and shelter. Stay away from overhangs, and never seek a rock that requires any sort of elaborate plan to retrieve. Be especially careful when collecting rocks in areas where poisonous reptiles and arachnids reside. When these creatures are disturbed, their bite can be swift and painful, their venom irritating and possibily life-threatening if an allergic reaction occurs.

Finally, the Pauite Indians believed that when they took a gift from the earth, they should return the favor. Although you may feel silly following such a practice as you collect rocks, the best present you can leave behind is to fill in any holes that have resulted from your rock harvesting. Leave no mark from your presence, and you have given back to nature in kindness and respect.

SAND AND CLAY

Less prevalent than rocks and stones in the wild, but still more widespread than other natural materials, is earth in its many forms, including sand and clay. Each can be used by itself or with other natural raw materials to create a variety of crafts.

Sand is the best example of rock that is not hard and does not hold its shape. Actually, sand is made up of bits or grains from older, solid rocks that have been weathered and worn into pieces over time. The largest pieces of sand are called pebbles; when great numbers of pebbles are mixed with sand grains they form coarse, loose rock known as gravel. Deposits of sand and gravel are formed from water soaking into the ground, which causes rocks such as granite to decay; from ancient glaciers, which broke off stones and then ground them into pieces, mixing them with large stones and clay; and, in and near rivers and seas, from the sand being separated from the gravel, resulting in beds of sea-made sand or sandstone, which contains very few pebbles and almost no clay. Sandy beaches, seaside dunes, and deserts are actually hills and ridges of such marine sand that have been piled up by the wind.

Sand is a resource that has been mined for years and can be found in such everyday things as concrete and plaster. The best grades of sand have been used for centuries to make glass for fine mirrors and tableware. Very little sand can be used in its natural state, as it comes out of the ground; most has to be washed to get rid of clay or mud, and then run through a series of screens to separate grains of different sizes. However, you can obtain natural sand for your crafting from a beach, from the desert, or along river banks, or you can purchase buckets of sand from a pet store, gravel yard, or foundry.

The biggest problem in creating with sand is that it does not hold together like clay. However, sand does come in a variety of textures and colors and, on its own, is a great natural abrasive for scouring pans while on camping trips, for keeping in your car or sprinkling on your front walk in the winter to prevent slipping on ice, and for holding back floodwaters.

Sand was long ago used as an art medium by American Indians, particularly the Navaho, who created temporary sand paintings for their religious ceremonies by sifting sands that had been dyed with traditional sacred colors—red, black, yellow, blue, and white—into patterns directly on the earth, where the sand paintings would then be blended back into the earth as part of the ritual. Such Native American sand paintings are recreated today by contemporary Indian artists on plywood or other durable (and portable) materials. You can make your own sand paintings in a similar fashion on a piece of wood or posterboard. To do so, first color the sand by soaking it for fifteen minutes in a solution of hot liquid dye or, for a more natural appearance, combine small quantities of the sand with ground cloves (for a dark brown color), cinnamon (for light brown), paprika (for red), cornmeal (for yellow), wheat flour (for buff), white flour (for white), or ground colored chalks (for a variety of colors). Sketch your design on the display board to plan for the positioning of sand colors on the finished art. Paint glue on one color section at a time, and then gently sprinkle the appropriately colored sand onto that section. Wait until each section is dry before painting a new section in order to keep your sand colors from blending. Continue until your sand painting is finished, then spray the finished painting with clear varnish to make it more durable.

❧

Clay is quite different from sand; when it is wet, you will be able to roll it around in the palm of your hand without it falling apart like dirt or sand. Also, if you poke your finger into a mass of it, your finger impression will remain. Native clay (not clay purchased from an art supply shop) is actually a rock made up of particles so tiny that they can hardly be seen. These fine particles of earth are suspended in water and found in natural deposits underground; good places to look for clay are along banks that have been cut away for construction or along stream and river beds.

Colors and textures of clay will vary, depending on the type of clay it is. White China clay, or kaolin, is the purest variety of clay, formed where veins of coarse granite were changed by water soaking into the ground or by steam that came from molten rock below the surface. This smooth, fine-grained clay remains white even after it is fired (heated in a kiln) and may be mixed with other substances to make dishes (hence the name "china" for dinnerware). Common clay, which is generally bluish-gray in color, is mined from shale deposits, or areas where the clay has been firmly packed into layers. Most common clay contains iron minerals that turn buff or brownish red when they become very hot; both common clay and shale are used to make bricks and tiles for buildings. Fire clay is a mixture of kaolin, common clay, sand, and other substances; bricks made with fire clay are buff or brownish yellow, very heavy, and can stand a great deal of heat without breaking or crumbling. Because of this, such bricks are predominantly used in fireplaces, kilns, and furnaces.

To collect clay, go out into the wild (or even your own backyard) with a small shovel and heavy-duty sealable plastic bags in which to keep the clay moist until you're ready to use it. Before working with the clay, be sure to pick out debris such as sticks, rocks, and bits of plants. Place the clay in a bucket and cover with water. Let stand overnight, then pour the wet mixture through a course screen, massaging lumps of clay through the holes as you remove smaller bits of debris. Squeeze out excess water from the strained clay, roll into smaller workable balls of clay, and then return to the plastic bags until needed. Later on, you can shape the clay into a variety of objects, including clay pots like those once made by the Native Americans.

ANCESTRAL NATURAL CREATIVITY CHALLENGE:

CLAY PINCH POT/NATURAL KILN

Crafting with clay requires that the clay first be worked to a consistency similar to that of bread dough, which means it must feel slightly spongy to the touch but not sticky. If the clay starts to crack as you work with it, it is too dry—you need to add more water; if the clay sticks to your hands, it is too wet—you need to pat it out for a few minutes on newspapers.

Massage the dough and knead it until it feels uniformly moist. Then form the moist clay into a ball, and push one thumb into the center of the clay without going all the way through the clay. Cup one hand underneath the clay, and use the other to slowly turn the clay as you pinch the sides between your thumb and forefinger. The opening of the pot will get larger and larger until the shape of the pinch pot is formed.

clay pinch pot

You can scratch a design into the sides of your pinch pot with a sharp twig if you like. Allow the pot to dry before you place it into a natural kiln. You can construct a natural kiln out of sand, brick, dry sawdust, dry twigs and grasses, and dry leaves or dry hay. To make the kiln, first dig a hole in the ground deep enough to cover your pinch pot. Line the hole with sand. Place the pot in the hole, then cover the pot with layers of sawdust and small, dry twigs. Top this with sawdust, then add a layer of dry hay or dry leaves and twigs until the hole is filled. Place brick or rocks around the top of the mound of layered, flammable materials in order to prevent the fire from spreading. Then light the mound and allow the fire to burn slowly. Let the fire cool completely before removing your pot.

Such raw natural materials as rocks, sand, clay, and even plain old dirt have been used by America's ancestors in numerous and wonderous ways for centuries—and have stood the test of time in their durability. Houses made using a process called rammed earth, which were built in America in the 1700s, are still in use today, as well as sod homes (used extensively on the prairies) and adobe structures. Such houses were constructed in complete harmony with the earth; the structure as well as everything in them was organic.

Lest you think that you have strayed far today from those days of all-organic housing and living, take some time to experiment with all the wonderful materials that are readily available and accessible from the wild earth. What you will find are many unique and rewarding ways in which to exhibit your natural creativity.

Exercising Your Wild-Earth Natural Creativity

1. The Japanese know about the wisdom in stones; they actually shop for stones in stores that sell them in sizes ranging from small pebbles to enormous boulders. Shop around in nature for your own stones that have interesting shapes and colors. Arrange them in a wooden bowl or around the base of a potted plant. Position a candle in the "bowl" of a stone or plant a small garden in the depression. Collect a large amount of smooth, intermediate-size pebbles to simulate a stream bed "flowing" through your garden. Harvest larger stones to make a rock garden. Locate round flat stones, paint sporty designs on them, and then package them as a gift for a young person who enjoys skipping stones.

2. With a group of friends, neighbors, or family members, create an outdoor meeting place out of large rocks that can be used by everyone as a place to sit and chat with others or for personal reflection. Hunt for and then carefully transport boulders from another location to the central meeting place, or reposition nearby boulders to form a circle or semi-circle in a part-sun/part-shade space. Decorate the space with wildflowers, herbs, bird feeders, a birdbath, wind chimes, rock art, and so on.

3. Make a stone arrow point (see Chapter 1, "Ancestral Natural Creativity Challenge: Arrow Points"). Then handpaint the point and use a leather cord to create a stone arrowhead pendant.

4. Create a nutcracker set out of one larger, flat base stone (on which to rest the nut) and a smaller, easy-to-hold cracking stone (with which to crack the nut). Look for stones that are attractive as well as offer creative adaptations to the function of being a nutcracker, such as a base stone that has a "storage-tray" depression to store nuts to be cracked or a natural trough in which to place a nut meat pick, or a cracking stone with a shape that suggests a particular nut (which you can then also paint to look like this nut, to further identify its purpose).

5. Many early paints and pigments were extracted from rocks; colored rocks were crushed and then mixed with water and animal fats. Iron oxide, for example, produced red, which can today be replicated even in city environments with old pieces of broken, soft brick.

You can also look in the wild for banks of crumbling rock, which are good sources of soft stones that produce a variety of colors. Place the softer rock (or piece of brick) on a flat stone, then grind a small amount of the soft rock with the hard stone. As the soft rock crumbles, add some water and vegetable oil, continuing to grind and mix the materials together. When the pigment has reached a spreadable consistency, use your fingers, live twigs cut from bushes or from short-bristled pine trees, or a store-bought paintbrush to create drawings on light-colored rocks that have a flat surface. Protect your finished art from rain or moisture by spraying with a light mist of fixative from an art-supply store. In making your drawing more permanent, however, the texture and color may be altered by the spray.

6. Make a "stone fruit" fruit bowl out of different sizes of round and smooth stones, in shapes that replicate real fruit—apples, oranges, grapes, lemons, limes, grapefruit, and so on. Then paint each stone fruit with the appropriate fruit color. Glue on stick stems and real leaves. When the paint is dry, polish with vegetable oil to add a shine. Arrange in a display in a bowl or basket.

7. Charcoal is the most available nontoxic material form of the color black for rock sketching. Do not use charcoal briquettes, however, which are manufactured materials that contain toxic bonding agents and igniters. Instead, make your own natural charcoal from a wood fire; be sure to put out the fire before all the wood burns to ash. You can sketch and draw with small, sharp pieces of this natural charcoal as well as with charcoal sticks purchased from an art supply store. To make black pigment, simply grind the charcoal and combine it with a little water and vegetable oil.

8. Make a **sand candle** by first filling a box or large bowl with sand, then making a depression (mold) of any size in the sand in which to pour hot candle wax. The depression can be finger-sized, for example, which will result in a short, narrow candle; the size of a flower pot for a wider candle; or an

sand candle

abstract shape, which will give the look of an object carved from sandstone or even dug up from an ancient ruin. Hang a candle wick over the center of the depression with a twig. Pour the hot wax into the mold. When the wax is completely dry, scoop the candle from its bed and brush away the loose sand.

9. Create your own desert dish garden by using interesting rocks you find, sand you collect, and succulents and cactus plants. Landscape by building a rock tower or distant "mountain" out of sandstone and other rocks that are glued together.

10. Make a wind chime by kiln-firing a number of oddly shaped clay pieces (be sure to make a hole in the pieces before firing). String the pieces together and hang from a tree so they will make musical contact with the help of a light wind or breeze.

9

WILD HOLIDAYS: *Celebrating with Natural Creativity*

Four times during the summer the community gathered to celebrate the maturation of the plantings, with the Green Corn ceremony held just before the harvest and marking the New Year. Everyone gathered to fast, pray, and dance their appreciation of the corn while it was alive and growing in the fields. The last rite was held in the fall when dancers, masked as animals, sanctified the community's economic shift from farming to hunting. Through participation in this ritual series, tribes were able to define their membership and assure continuity.

—writer DAVID HURST THOMAS et al., from *The Native Americans*

A lovely thing about Christmas is that it's compulsory, like a thunderstorm, and we all go through it together. —American humorist and author GARRISON KEILLOR, from *Leaving Home*

LONG BEFORE NATIVE AMERICAN TRIBES were formed in America—tribes were really organizations that were created following disruptions by New World explorers and the influx of European diseases that decimated great numbers of Indians—parts of ancient America were settled by loosely knit groups of Indians whose common identity was created and maintained during the celebration of rituals. These periodic celebrations, in which a whole community or several communities might join, were intended to renew the world with which the group of people were familiar and, as well, their connectedness with all living things within that world. For example, farming communities would celebrate, through rituals, the arrival of spring rain, the time of planting, and times of harvest; hunter-gatherers would hold ritual celebrations to welcome the annual run of fish, the passing of migrating herds, or a bountiful hunt.

Such rituals served to unite diverse peoples, at least during the times in which these celebrations were held, in shared acts of communion that minimized their differences in language, culture, food, housing, and ways of living and, instead, focused on their common identity through joyful and enriching celebrations. So, too, do today's ritualistic celebrations—communal holidays such as Thanksgiving as well as personal holidays such as birthdays and anniversaries—unite families and extended families; friends and friends of friends; companions and life partners; neighbors and neighborhoods; coworkers and teammates; church congregations and interfaith communities; and members of social, civic, professional, and self-help organizations in joyful and enriching unions and reunions. Because ancient tradition has long held that gifts be exchanged or shared during such ritualistic celebrations and because ancient traditional gifts were hand-fashioned out of whatever could be hunted, harvested, grown, or gathered from the natural environment in which the ancient peoples lived, exercising your natural creativity today during holidays and other celebrations involves the challenge of discovering unique ways to gift-craft with nature's many raw materials in ways that capture the essence, or spirit, of the particular holiday being celebrated or the special person being honored.

In essence, anything that you have created thus far in your exploration of natural creativity is an appropriate gift to share with others or to give to someone special during a holiday or celebration: an acorn-and-pinecone wreath at Christmas, a fresh floral bouquet cut from your backyard wildflower garden or a fragrant potpourri made out of flowers and herbs you have gathered and dried for Easter, a mobile you have delicately fashioned out of seashells you have collected for a family reunion at the family's seaside cottage, or a

a fish to celebrate

personalized rock totem you have painted for a best friend's birthday. But there are many other ways in which you can naturally evoke the spirit of a particular holiday or occasion. What follows are some of the more common holidays traditionally celebrated throughout the year and some of the naturally creative ways in which you can commemorate them through decorations and/or gifts.

New Year's Eve/Day (December 31/January 1) Most people traditionally look forward to a new start—a clean slate—at the beginning of a new year by making one or more New Year's resolutions. But the majority of resolutions made for the new year can be punitive rather than positive, or they may focus on what is wrong rather than on what is right. So, by yourself, with an intimate partner, or with family members, create a Nature New Year Collage—a visual representation of a hope or dream and how such a hope or dream can come true with the help of the natural world. For example, if it is your hope to lose weight, instead of focusing on diet plans, ideal weights, or the enviable size and shape of supermodels, shift your focus in your collage to the natural world, which provides you with good foods such as fruits and vegetables, fresh air in which to exercise, challenging mountains to climb or trails to hike, and so on.

To create such a collage, first gather scissors, poster board or construction paper, and glue, and then assemble the natural raw materials you have previously collected: dried flowers and herbs, seashells, twigs, feathers, and so on. You can also use photographs you have taken, postcards, and natural scenes cut out of magazines—anything you feel would be suitable to use in your Nature New Year Collage. Then take time to reflect on a deep desire you have for yourself—not something that needs to be improved but, rather, something you feel would enhance the quality of your life. Begin to assemble the collage, but refrain from forcing your design; instead, let your creativity flow. When you have completed your Nature New Year Collage, display it or keep it handy for frequent consultation during the upcoming year.

Groundhog Day (February 2) Create a rock **groundhog** out of paint and a rock that is an appropriate size and shape for the animal. Display the groundhog outside your front door

Woodchuck, or Groundhog

on February 2 each year. If your groundhog sees his shadow on that day, tradition dictates that he return underground because winter is not yet over, so you must remove the groundhog from display. However, if the groundhog does not see his shadow, leave him on display to welcome the forthcoming spring.

Valentine's Day (February 14) Create a traditional "tree proclamation" of love to give to a special person in your life. First find a branch or log that is approximately four to six inches in diameter and still has its bark well attached. Cut from this near-dead or dead wood a portion no more than eight inches in length. Make sure both ends of the cut piece are level so the wood will not wobble when displayed on a flat surface. When the bark and wood are completely dry, carve into the bark a proclamation of your love for your special someone— a heart with both your initials in it, for example, or the date of your anniversary. Wrap the log in a bright red bow, then present it to the one you love.

St. Patrick's Day (March 17) Create a "meadow" of four-leaf clovers out of a number of small round pebbles on each of which you paint a lucky four-leaf clover. Scatter the clover stones in a large clay pot base, on top of a bed of dirt, moss, and lichens, to make a year-round, living good-luck terrarium.

Easter (date varies; falls in late March or early April) Bring along an empty egg carton while you search for and gather a dozen egg-shaped rocks of uniform size. Wash and dry the rocks at home, then decorate the rocks with paint to look like colorful Easter eggs. Hide the "eggs" around your house or yard for a family Easter-egg hunt, or display them in a basket for a festive table centerpiece. Use the carton to store the rock eggs safely until next year's holiday celebration.

Earth Day (April 22) Make a set of four nature coasters to display in your home on Earth Day or to give to a special person as a reminder of earth's valuable presence in everyday life. Cut scrap pieces of wood to a size that is large enough to comfortably rest a coffee mug or beer stein. You may choose to make the pieces of wood in the set uniform (all one size and shape) or you can vary the shapes within the set (one round, one square, one triangular, and one diamond-shaped, for example).

If you have not previously done so, collect and dry a variety of sizes and shapes of leaves, then glue the leaves onto each piece of wood in interesting and creative arrangements. Place a piece of waxed paper over the glued leaves, then stack a pile of books on top of the waxed paper. When the leaves have dried, carefully peel away the waxed paper. On the back of each coaster, indicate the type of leaves that are shown on the front. Then cover each leaf coaster with three coats of varnish, applying each new coat after the previous coat has dried.

Mother's Day (second Sunday in May) Frame a favorite outdoor picture from your family's past to give to your mother. Collect four sticks that are about the same width, then cut them so they are the same length. Lash them together with an enduring natural raw material (such as a vine), a natural fiber string, or an attractive leather or imitation leather cord. Then cut a piece of posterboard to a size slightly larger than the frame that has been created by the sticks. Center the photograph you would like to frame on the posterboard, then glue the two together. Edge the sides of the front of the posterboard (the side that displays the picture) with glue, then firmly adhere to the backs of the sticks (where the lashing is tied together). Nail a picture-hanging hook on the back—and in the center—of one of the sticks.

Memorial Day (last Monday in May) The four years of the fiercely fought Civil War—from 1861 to 1865—cost the lives of many thousands of vital and brave American souls. Shortly after the war ended, a custom grew in the Southern states of strewing flowers on the graves of Confederate soldiers who had been lost in that conflict. Today Memorial Day, also known as Decoration Day (for Union soldiers) and Confederate Memorial Day (for Confederate soldiers), is a time when the custom of leaving flowers on the gravesites of war veterans is traditionally observed.

You can create a unique and beautiful red-white-and-blue floral display to leave at the gravesite of a war veteran from your family or community out of dried wildflowers, herbs, and/or wild grasses that you have collected and then dyed with natural dyes. To make a brilliant white, lightly mist the dried floral piece or pieces with water and then dredge in white flour to coat. Shake off any excess flour. To make a bright blue and a striking red use a natural berry dye made out of, respectively, blueberries and raspberries or strawberries. Place the fresh berries in a cooking pot with water—the less water you use, the deeper the dye will be—and bring to a boil. Reduce the heat, cover, and simmer for about an hour, stirring occasionally. Remove the mixture from the heat and cool. Then strain the berries to leave behind the liquid dye. Soak the dried floral piece or pieces in their respective dyes; allow to dry before arranging together in a simple glass jar for a Memorial Day display that you can place near a headstone.

Father's Day (third Sunday in June) Make your father a natural pen and pencil holder for his office or home-office desk. First locate an interesting piece of near-dead wood, about the size of your hand, that is less like a stick or a branch in shape and more like a chunk or even a round piece of wood. Allow the wood to dry, then strip it of its bark and sand to remove any rough edges. Find out which way it rests easily on a desk top without wobbling, then sand, trim, or cut along this bottom edge to make the holder more stable. Drill a few holes equal to the width of a pen or pencil into the top of the wood, then prop a couple of brand-new pens or pencils into the holes for display.

Independence Day (Fourth of July) Bake and then decorate a holiday cake in any number of patriotic designs using white (white frosting), red (strawberries or raspberries), and blue (blueberries). Or create an All-American Parfait in a parfait glass or other tall glass by layering vanilla ice cream, blueberries, and strawberries or raspberries.

Labor Day (first Monday in September) At one time, "Labor's

Holiday," or what is now known as Labor Day, was a day on which workers all across the country put aside their tasks. Now, however, it is considered to be the last—and most frantic—day in which to complete back-to-school shopping, end-of-vacation unpacking, and summer-home or cabin closing.

Use as little creative energy as possible on this traditional holiday of rest by exploring what you can easily make out of burdocks. Burdocks, also known as burrs or cockleburrs, inspired the invention of Velcro, which has made everyday life less laborious for everyone. To collect **burdocks,** walk through an overgrown field or pasture and gather them by hand from the plants or on your clothes as you walk through the plants. When you return home, stick the burdocks together to create animals, trees, a bird's nest, or other nature **sculptures.**

A cockleburr "cactus"

Columbus Day (second Monday in October) Construct the Santa Maria, the Nina, and the Pinta—or an entire fleet of **sailing vessels**—out of walnut shells, pine pitch, twigs, and birch bark. To make two boats, first carefully crack open a walnut shell to make two halves. Clean out the meat and fiber from each half-shell. From the piece of birch bark that you have collected, cut two sails that are appropriately sized to the dimensions of each ship. Make two small cuts in each sail—one near the top and one near

A walnut shell boat

the bottom—so that a twig, which will function as the ship's mast, easily slides through the holes. Bend each bark sail outward from the twig to give the appearance of a gust of wind filling the sails. Then spread pine pitch, clear glue, or even gum across the bottom of each shell. Place the bottom end of the twig mast into the sticky substance. Allow the pitch to dry, then display your finished vessels on a mirror on a table top.

Veteran's Day (November 11) On November 11, 1918, German

representatives signed an armistice that ended the exhaustive first World War. For about forty years thereafter, November 11 was celebrated as Armistice Day, (in some states it was called Victory Day); today November 11 is known as Veterans Day and honors all the men and women who have bravely served in the armed forces.

Prepare a simple patriotic commemorative to leave at the gravesite of a former member of the armed forces. Lightly sand the inside of a large clam shell to prepare the surface for painting. Then paint an American flag, an insignia of a particular branch of the military, or another patriotic symbol or message inside the shell.

Halloween (October 31) When hollowed out, many vegetables can be used as serving bowls, such as for a festive Halloween soup made out of pumpkins, walnuts, and maple syrup and then served in a pumpkin tureen.

ANCESTRAL NATURAL CREATIVITY CHALLENGE:

BLACK AND ORANGE HALLOWEEN SOUP

Roast a small, whole, washed **pumpkin** that is no more than twelve inches in diameter in a 325° oven for about an hour, or until the skin wrinkles and can easily be pierced with a sharp utensil. Remove from the oven, and cut the pumpkin open. (Be careful—the insides will be piping hot!) Spoon out the seeds first—save them for later if you wish to toast them. Then spoon out the pumpkin meat

into a saucepan. Mash the pumpkin with a cup of chopped black walnuts and maple syrup (to taste). Add about a quart of water, or a suitable amount for making the desired soup consistency. Mix well, then simmer in a covered pan for as little as five minutes before eating.

Prior to serving, hollow out and thoroughly wash a medium-size raw pumpkin. Make sure that you do not pierce the outer skin. Carve a wide top on the pumpkin, then pour in the hot soup. Decorate the base of the pumpkin with fall leaves, dried flowers and herbs, corn husks, gourds, and miniature pumpkins. Use a ladle to serve the soup (serves four to six people).

Thanksgiving (fourth or last Thursday in November) In 1621, in the little colony at Plymouth, Massachusetts, Pilgrims had been in the New World for nearly a year. All summer long the fields had been tended with great care and then watched over with even greater anxiety, for the colonists' lives depended on the bounty of the upcoming harvest to help them survive the harsh New England winter. Because the summer crops were fruitful beyond all expectation, one day late in the fall, Governor Bradford sent four men into the forests to shoot wild birds. "We will hold a harvest of thanksgiving," he told them, and then invited the Indians who had been friendly to them to rejoice with the white settlers. The Indians came bearing gifts of venison, and the harvest feast lasted three days.

This was the first Thanksgiving Day celebrated in America; as new colonies settled the land, the custom of a yearly Thanksgiving spread throughout the country. In 1864, President Abraham Lincoln issued a presidential proclamation appointing Thanksgiving as a holiday on the fourth or last Thursday of November. But it was George Washington who perfectly expressed the spirit of the day in his Thanksgiving Proclamation in 1789:

> Whereas it is the duty of all nations to acknowledge the providence of Almighty God, to obey his will, to be grateful for his benefits, and humbly to implore his protection, aid and favors. . . . Now, therefore, I do recommend and assign Thursday, the 26th day of November next, to be devoted by the people of these States to the service of that great and glorious Being, who is the Beneficent Author of all the good that was, that is or that will be; that we may then all unite in rendering unto him our sincere and humble thanks for his kind care and protection of the people of this country, and for all the great and various favors which he has been pleased to confer upon us.

This Thanksgiving, prior to celebrating, visit a local library to locate a stuffing, vegetable, or side-dish recipe that was once traditionally prepared by Native Americans or early Americans, such as baked butternut squash, cranberry and walnut sauce, or hickory-nut corn pudding. Then add this dish to your own Thanksgiving menu, or prepare it to share with others at a communal meal.

Christmas (December 25) Make a milkweed-pod star by threading or firmly gluing together each base of five dried and empty milkweed pods so the bases fit snugly to one another and form a center to the star while the pods radiate outward to form the five points. Tie off the thread, string, or other material used (such as yarn). Use glue to adhere sand or bits of mica to the star to make it glitter in the light. Or push a white or blue Christmas light into the center to create a window star for each window in your home. You can string together a series of lit milkweed-pod stars as a glorious garland to adorn a mantelpiece, stairway handrail, or door frame.

Kwanza (December 26) As ancient as many holidays are, so, too, is the wearing of jewelry during such celebrations. Ever since people first began to wear jewelry, natural things were strung together and worn around the neck and wrists: shells, teeth, tusks, bones, and seeds. Collect a variety of seeds from melons, squash, and pumpkins to make an **African seed necklace.** Wash and dry the seeds. If desired, dye the seeds with food coloring or natural dyes such as those made from berry juices. Allow the dyed seeds to dry before stringing. Thread a needle with sewing thread, tie one end securely, then sew the seeds onto the thread to reach a desired length and/or pattern. Cut the thread, then tie off the other end. Knot the ends of the thread together so the necklace will slip over your head easily.

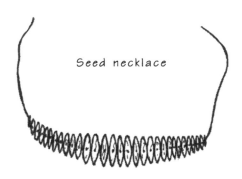

Seed necklace

The holidays you celebrate with the rest of the world and with other Americans; the special days you commemorate with people who share your culture and your religious beliefs or who live in your community and your neighborhood; and the significant times you joyously participate in with your life partner, your friends, and your family members hold a special significance that is best commemorated when you give a gift that comes from your heart and your handiwork. Using natural raw materials in your celebratory crafting is not only rewarding but symbolizes the ancient rituals from which many of today's celebrations originated.

Celebrating with Your Natural Creativity

1. Celebrate the first day of spring, first day of summer, first day of autumn, and first day of winter by displaying on your mantel, in the center of your dining room table, or on your front door a collection of natural raw materials that evoke the spirit of the season—daffodils grown from bulbs in spring, an array of seashells in summer, fall leaves in autumn, or holly boughs or pinecones in winter.

2. Carve a variety of fruits and/or vegetables out of a soft wood, then paint each to resemble the particular fruit or vegetable whose shape it represents—a peach, a pear, an apple, a carrot, a banana, and so on. Design unique ways to display bunches of these wood "edibles"—a bunch of grapes, for instance, or radishes. Arrange the wood creations in a seasonal centerpiece in your home, or give a different edible to the same person each year for a unique collectible gift-giving tradition.

3. Make a festive jingle bell–pinecone winter door chime out of pinecones and jingle bells, which can be purchased from a crafts store in a variety of sizes and tones. After you collect the pinecones from outdoors, bring them inside and allow them to dry. Then use an awl, nail, or drill to puncture a hole at the base (the wider end) of each pinecone. Next, use leather or imitation leather craft cord to string together a garland that has alternating pine cones and jingle bells. When your garland reaches the desired length, tie off each end securely, then hang from a doorknob or across the top of a door.

4. To add a natural touch to the simple present of a published book, make a nature bookmark to slip inside the book before giving. First cut a strip of heavy posterboard or oaktag that is at least one inch wide and slightly longer than the size of the book for which you are making the bookmark. Then, paint a thin coating of glue onto the back of a dried flower, a bird feather, a leaf, or other natural raw material you have collected. Gently press the natural material onto the bookmark. If desired, add sketches or other creative touches to either or both sides of the bookmark.

5. One of the nicest and more personal presents you can make and give is a box of handmade nature stationery. Many stationery stores sell sets of blank cards and envelopes, as well as sheets of plain stationery paper and matching/coordinating envelopes by the pound. Once you have selected the appropriate notepaper, all you need to do is gather and press-dry a variety of "flat" flowers (such as daisies), herbs, ferns, and leaves. Once the floral gatherings have dried, create each sheet of nature notepaper by painting the back of a selected floral sample with glue, and then gently pressing it onto the top or center of a sheet of stationery or a note card. Or create a floral border of several dried flowers that runs down one side of a sheet of stationery. Place a sheet of waxed paper over each note card or sheet of stationery, and insert in the center of a large book to dry overnight. Pair the nature note cards or stationery with the envelopes, and then tie the entire package together with a pretty bow.

6. Create a Celebration Tree that can be displayed during any holiday, seasonal celebration, or commemorative event, depending on how you decorate it. Find a branch with an interesting shape— and without any leaves or needles—and stick it into a clay pot, plastic-lined basket, or other interesting container that is filled with sand or small pebbles to hold the stick firmly in place. Then decorate the branches of the tree with items you make, with strings of lights, or with things you collect from nature.

7. For any gift you give, instead of using store-bought wrapping paper, make your own wrapping paper out of plain brown paper embellished with glued-on dried flowers; instead of curling ribbon, use natural cordage or all-natural twine, accented with a seashell or bird feather that is secured into the knot; instead of manufactured gift tags, make your own out of birch bark or large dried leaves.

8. To add a unique natural touch to a special meal, make Nature Napkin Rings. Save the cardboard inner tubes from toilet paper and paper towel rolls or purchase strong cardboard mailing tubes. Cut two-inch long pieces from the rolls or tubes, then glue bark or twigs of approximately the same length onto the cardboard. Roll a cloth napkin lengthwise; then insert it into a Nature Napkin Ring.

9. Light a holiday dinner table with candles of various sizes and shapes that have each been made more festive with a candle ring of braided wild grasses and fragrant herbs wrapped around its base.

10. Collect a large bundle of wheat and other dried straws, cut portions of the bundles to different lengths, and then arrange the bundle in a tight sheaf. Secure with twine or wire, then wrap with a seasonal, holiday, or other celebratory bow and display on your front door, on a mantelpiece, or on a living room or hallway wall. Change the bow, depending on the celebration or time of year.

10

WILD LIVING:
Natural Creativity
in Daily Life

Hoping to help our daughters develop an appreciation of nature, my husband and I took them camping. After we arrived at the campsite and unloaded our gear, we all set to work. My husband had the girls gather pine needles to make soft "beds." Then he instructed them to bring rocks to form a circle in a cool stream. We placed our perishables inside. My husband explained that this would be our "refrigerator." Next, we made a "stove" by making a ring of stones topped with a grate. The girls were impressed and excited. Our five-year-old smiled up at her father. "If we get more rocks, Daddy," she asked, "will you make a TV?"

—contributed by BARBARA BOCK to *Reader's Digest,* June 1996

Day AFTER DAY, MANKIND, animals, birds, insects, reptiles, amphibians, fish, plants, rocks, earth, water, and air all successfully cohabitate on and share the bounties of Planet Earth. Yet although mankind is dependent on all these natural things for sustenance and daily living, nothing in the natural world is dependent on mankind for maintaining its own existence. What this means is that you need the natural world more than it needs you. You need the natural world not just for its nonliving elements—**the oil that comes gushing out of the ground,** for instance, or the water that comes rushing down the mountainside—but, as well, for all of its living things. You eat (or may choose not to eat) animals, birds, and fish. You eat many types of root vegetables and leafy vegetables; the unripe seeds of

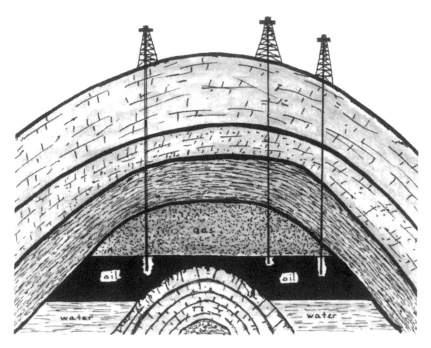

Tapping an oil pool.

peas and beans; cultivated and wild fruits; grains; and rices. You use herbs and spices to add zest and flavor to your culinary creations. You enjoy wines and spirits made from corn, rice, and wheat, as well as natural mild stimulants such as tea and coffee. You wash your hair, soften your skin, lubricate your beard, enhance your smell, make up your face, and cleanse and beautify your body with the help of animals and plants. You stay warm outdoors in the winter and sleep comfortably in your bed at night because of animals and birds. Pharmaceuticals made from herbs and medicinal plants help you combat illness, ease pain, soothe stress, and maintain overall health and well-being. Rushes and reeds make functional and decorative baskets; clay forms bricks, planting pots, pottery, and dishware. Ores, when smelted, make steel, iron, and other durable metals for automobiles, skyscrapers, airplanes, and ships as well as the cans from which you drink beverages. Trees provide you with furniture as well as the house in which you use the furniture.

Because you need the natural world more than it needs you, cultivating and preserving as much of this natural world is integral not just for the quality of your daily life but, as well, for the enhancement of daily living through the naturally creative ways in which you put nature to functional as well as enjoyable use. The best place to start cultivating and preserving the natural world is where you reside. This ensures a personal bounty of natural raw materials that can supplement, or even supply you with, the materials to experiment with as you explore a variety of natural creativity projects.

❧

"Living with the earth" is a phrase most often employed by those who forsake city living in order to live more simply, surrounded by acres of undisturbed nature. "Getting back to nature" is another phrase that often signals the desire to eliminate all or nearly all processed, packaged, and manufactured goods used in daily life in favor of those things that can be found on or in the earth. Neither one of these, however, is a realistic option for most people, even those who strongly desire to develop and hone their ability to successfully adapt nature to creative and functional everyday living—

as American Indians and early settlers once did—through the use of nature's raw materials. Making such a radical relocation to **live with the earth** often involves giving up a job that has a dependable salary and a high level of security; uprooting children from their familiar neighborhoods, friends, and school systems; and adding distance between friends and family. As well, "getting back to nature" is not as easy as it sounds. It requires not just a deliberate shift in forsaking goods formerly purchased and services once employed but, as well, immersion in studies that range from basic nutritional needs to more complex survival skills.

Devising ways to live more "in the wild"—or, at least, a bit closer to nature—can be particularly frustrating when living in a high-rise apartment building in a city, for this way of life pretty much eliminates the cultivation of anything bigger than a pot garden on a terrace or a window herb box. And while living in the suburbs offers more land on which to home-grow vegetables, fruits, and flowers, rarely is there enough time to tend to the garden. Sometimes, too, the initial excitement experienced during the first planting and harvest from a vegetable garden, the creation of a rock garden, the digging of a fish pond, or the keeping of bees for a fresh store of honey fades quickly away upon the realization of how much time such things take to maintain. Over the years, too, such ongoing maintenance can exact a physical toll on an aching back.

Many back-to-nature, living-with-the-earth home-based projects require a certain degree of beginning as well as ongoing knowledge. Growing any living thing—wildflowers, herbs, perennials, annuals, bulbs, fruit trees, flowering trees, bushes, and so on—requires that you know about each plant's life cycle, or habit of growth. You also need to know about a plant's hardiness, or its resistance to certain environmental factors, such as cold temperatures. (The U.S. Department of Agriculture has divided the United States into numbered climate zones; each of these zones is used when describing a plant's hardiness. A zone 8 plant, for example, can only be grown in the southern United States, below Tennessee, Arkansas, Oklahoma, and the northern half of Texas.) Additionally, you need to know how to care for each particular plant: how to prepare its bed, how and when to fertilize it, what its water needs are, what sun requirements it has, when it blooms, how it must be pruned, how to divide it and when to transplant it, and so on.

And yet, despite all these considerations and cautions, it really takes little to add a bit of wild living to your everyday life. The idea is not for you to give up all or even any modern conveniences or ways of doing things or to pull up roots and relocate in order to live physically closer to nature but, instead, to learn about and then experience for yourself the simplicity, beauty, and value of some forgotten natural arts—or to even invent some natural arts yourself with nature's raw materials. *The point of wild living is not to abandon the modern world but to live more fully within it by becoming more aware of the historical perspective nature has had in craftsmaking, and then to integrate some of these natural raw materials into crafting in your modern life.*

Natural creativity in everyday life encourages you to develop crafting skills as well as to deepen your awareness of the meaningful ways your ancestors used nature and crafting from nature to enhance their everyday living. For example, centuries ago, plants offered mankind a floating, flexible substance that allowed them to explore the waters that had once bounded them to their lands. From the first hollowed-out log came an opportunity for a new experience—a voyage of discovery that opened up new worlds not just to the travelers but to those on the shores that received the travelers.

Today, as naturalist and writer John McPhee has observed, "Travel by canoe is not a necessity, and will nevermore be the most efficient way to get from one region to another, or even from one lake to another—anywhere. A canoe trip has become simply a rite of oneness with certain terrain, a diversion off the field, an art performed not because it is a necessity but because there is value in the art itself." Just because some things from the past may no longer be necessary to the way you live your life does not mean that such things cannot be revisited from time to time, reused occasionally, reemployed every once in a while, or even reexperienced on a regular basis in your life today. A fire built in your fireplace can still provide warmth on a raw day, keep a kettle of soup warm, pop popcorn, or shine a light on a book. Just one vegetable grown in a home garden plot or balcony pot can dress up an evening's salad or be canned to enjoy during the winter. A personal letter can still be handwritten, decorated with a pressed flower, and posted to arrive at a friend's house. A musical instrument can still be whittled from a piece of wood. Pine needles can still be gathered to make a soft forest bed. **Animals can still be tracked through the woods by the prints,** markings, and scat they leave behind. The wind can still forewarn of a storm. A canoe can still take you to a midlake island or a distant shore.

Sketch of mink tracks,
fore and hind

Of course you can always turn on your furnace for heat, turn on your stove for cooking, or flick a switch for electricity by which to read a book. You can stop at a grocery store to pick up fresh, frozen, or canned vegetables. You can e-mail or fax a friend. You can purchase a finely crafted musical instrument or buy tickets for an evening at the symphony. You can take the time to pump air into a plastic-coated mattress or not even bother to go camping at all. You can visit animals in a zoo or watch their behaviors on a television program. You can turn on a weather radio or listen to the evening forecast rather than step outside to "feel" the weather yourself. You can rev up the motor on a boat or not even make the journey to a midlake island for a picnic on a fine summer day.

You always have the option of relying solely on modern technology. As well, you have the option of exploring, from time to time, your connection to nature through natural creativity crafting. While your life today may be more complicated than that of your ancient ancestors, beneath your civilized facade you are strikingly similar to them: you have the same needs, the same desires, and the same instincts as those who lived long before you. The main difference is that today, without natural creativity exercise, your senses are duller.

But when you allow yourself to explore and exercise your natural creativity, you forge an ongoing connection to nature and all of its wonderfully workable raw materials. More importantly, you enhance and expand the modern world by living more fully within its heritage. As naturalist and journalist Henry David Thoreau once wrote:

> We must learn to reawaken and keep ourselves awake, not by mechanical aids, but by an infinite expectation of the dawn, which does not forsake us in our soundest sleep. I know of no more encouraging fact than the unquestionable ability of man to elevate his life by a conscious endeavor. It is something to be able to paint a particular picture, or to carve a statue, and so to make a few objects beautiful, but it is more glorious to carve and paint the very atmosphere and medium through which we look, which morally we can do. To affect the quality of the day, that is the highest of arts.

Exercising Your Natural Creativity in Daily Life

1. Make an indoor sprouts garden for a fresh, nutritious, year-round complement to sandwiches, side dishes, omelets, and salads. There are a variety of methods you can use for sprouting. The easiest involves the purchase of a sprouting kit, which often comes with everything you need, including seeds, to start your fast-growing sprouts. You can also select your own seeds to sprout—mung beans, lentils, soybeans, sunflower seeds, pumpkin seeds, or the seeds of almost any grain such as wheat, alfalfa, barley, buckwheat, rye, and oat (each will have its own distinctive flavor).

First wash the seeds, and then let them soak overnight in water at room temperature. The next day, pour off the water and rinse the seeds thoroughly. Lay a couple of sheets of plain paper toweling on the bottom of an opaque mixing bowl (not clear glass) in order to keep the seeds in a dark environment. Spread the drained seeds in the bowl, blanket with a moist paper towel, then cover the bowl with a plate to keep out light. Store the covered bowl at room temperature. Each day, rinse the seeds three times. Change the paper toweling with each rinsing to soak up extra moisture. Mung beans will sprout quickly with this method, in about three or four days. Other seeds, particularly those that are hard and large, may take longer. Wait for the sprouts to grow to at least the length of the seeds—this indicates maturity—before using. Refrigerate the sprouts for up to a week.

2. Practice different methods of catching fish without a fishing pole and modern tackle—with just a hook and line as the American Indians once did. You can engage in skittering, which is done with a long stick or cane pole, a line about twelve feet long, and a medium-size, baited hook. Swing the baited line out and then "skitter" it along the edges of lily pads, logs, and other still areas in a pond or lake. The idea is to recreate natural water surface activity to attract the attention of a hungry pickerel or bass.

If you have access to a rowboat or canoe, you can put empty plastic water or milk jugs to good use by "jugging." Cap or cork the jugs securely so they will float. Tie onto each jug handle a fishing line about ten feet long. Equip each line with a baited hook and a sinker.

Row the boat into the middle of a pond or lake, then release the jugs. Sit tight, and keep an eye on the jugs. When the fish begin to bite, the jugs will bounce, spin, and exhibit other erratic movement. Simply paddle out to each jiggling jug and retrieve your catch. Such primitive fishing methods, as well as fishing with gear you make or find yourself, add to the fun and adventure of fishing.

3. If you have the space outdoors, plant and cultivate your own vine-growing ornamental gourds for a variety of naturally creative uses. Gourds are heat-loving plants that require plenty of sunshine and warmth. Sow the seeds about an inch deep in rich soil in a sunny location. The vines will grow freely on the ground or will create a natural screen along a trellis or fence. Although gourds grow in an endless array of unique shapes, they can also be shaped while growing. During the hottest part of the day, gently work the gourds with your fingers to achieve a particular shape. Or employ the Native American tradition of wrapping bandages snugly, but not too tightly, around the gourds (this is the way smoking pipes were created).

The resulting decorative gourds can be made into Native American objects such as dance rattles; exquisite vases, bowls, and dishes; **naturally watertight jugs** and containers; funnels; dippers and cups; candle holders and napkin rings; bird houses; and many more interesting and functional objects. Gourds can also be decorated with paint (spray with a fixative after the paint has dried) or waxed with floor wax and then polished to preserve the color and add luster.

Gourd water jugs

4. Create a "tussie-mussie" from what you grow in your own garden, from what you pick out in the wild, or from what you can gather at a farm stand that allows flower and herb cutting by the

pound. Tussie-mussies are carefully arranged, small bunches of herbs and blossoms in which every sprig chosen has symbolic, ancient, religious, or mythological meaning. In essence, tussie-mussies are floral messages that communicate how you feel to the recipient, based on the language of the flowers chosen: a get-well wish to someone who is ailing; a birthday wish of joy and happiness; a message of love and adoration; and so on.

To plan your tussie-mussie message, peruse books that detail herbal and floral meanings. While it is well known that the red rose says "I love you," virtually every flower, herb, tree, shrub, vine, and weed has its own meaning in floral language: ivy expresses friend-ship, for instance, while lamb's ear conveys gentleness, thyme courage and strength, yarrow good health, and zinnia thoughts of absent friends.

To make your tussie-mussie, first plan your message; then gather flowers and herbs that convey this sentiment. Tie the stems together with a natural vine, twine, or decorative ribbon to create the compact, communicative, hand-held bouquet.

5. Track an animal not for the purpose of catching up to it—ani-mals are professionals at avoiding mankind, and even the most accomplished tracker does not always get to see the animal being tracked—but so that you can learn something about the animal, such as its habits or what it needs from its habitat. The best time to track is in the winter, after a snowfall, when you can easily follow the movements of an animal thoroughout its environment; or following a heavy rain, when you can track an animal from the prints it makes in the softened ground.

As you track, try to discover both how and why the animal moves, from the tracks it has made. Does it leap, lope, run, walk, jump, or use a combination of these movements? Figure out if your animal likes to be solitary or enjoys the company of others. Try to find where the animal rests and where—and on what—it dines. Locate the nearest water source used by the animal. Through your tracking, consider where the animal might den, nest, burrow, or set-tle down to sleep.

6. Home brew your own beer, wine, brandy, or soda by using prepared kits or by taking a workshop in home-brewing offered by an adult-education program or local microbrewery.

7. Convert a spare room, attic space, or section of the basement into a natural-creativity studio for occasional experimentation with natural-creativity projects as well as for more serious exploration of crafting for the creation of items for sale to gift shops, for craft-show sale and exhibition, for studio display or art competition, or to begin a part-time home-order business.

8. Attract birds to your yard with store-bought feeders (to minimize squirrel and skunk interest) as well as feeding stations you make out of natural raw materials. You can grow sunflowers, for example, and then, after they have bloomed, hang the blossoms from trees. These **seed-filled blossoms** are adored by cardinals, jays, nuthatches, and titmice. By gathering birds in your yard, you will be rewarded not just by the songs and antics of the birds but also by their feathers, for use in a variety of craft projects.

Sunflower blossom
bird feeder

9. If you have been or anticipate being politely ushered out of your job, think about planting the seeds of a whole new business—one that may effectively use your workplace skills, capitalize on your creativity, and employ the use of nature in some way, shape, or form. For example, when a valued member of a management team at Digital Equipment Corporation in Massachusetts was offered an early retirement package prior to being laid off, he took the buyout offer, bid adieu to his $100,000-a-year salary, and founded Maine Bonsai Gardens. The former corporate manager used his manage-

ment skills as well as his creative energy and love of nature to start a greenhouse that specializes in the ancient Asian art form of bonsai. In its third year of business, Maine Bonsai Gardens grossed $300,000 in sales.

10. Every year, take a vacation that brings you in close contact with the natural world. Camp, hike, climb a mountain, canoe, rent a cottage by the ocean or a lake, or enroll in an outdoor workshop or adventure. Take advantage of this time outdoors to explore your natural surroundings. Learn what you can use from the natural materials that are readily available—a pile of pine needles placed under your sleeping bag, for instance, can be just as comfortable as an air mattress. Too, discover which "creature comforts" you can easily do without. Upon returning home, strive to make such nonessential items less important in your daily life. For example, read a book instead of mindlessly channel surfing; take your dog for a long walk in the woods rather than for a quick "business trip" around the block; or make a tasty homemade soup for dinner rather than heating the contents of store-bought cans.

Recommended Resources* for Natural Creativity

Aldrich, Dot. *Creating with Cattails, Cones and Pods*. Great Neck, N.Y.: Hearthside Press Inc., 1971.

Angier, Bradford. *Feasting Free on Wild Edibles*. Harrisburg, Pa.: Stackpole Books, 1972.

Bales, Suzanne Frutig. *Gifts From Your Garden: A Seasonal Album of Decorations and Keepsakes*. New York: Prentice Hall, 1992.

Bandi, Hans-Georg et al. *The Art of the Stone Age: Forty Thousand Years of Rock Art*. New York: Crown Publishers, Inc., 1961.

Beebe, William. *Unseen Life of New York as a Naturalist Sees It*. New York: Duell, Sloan, and Pearce, 1953.

The Best of Martha Stewart Living Handmade Christmas. New York: Clarkson-Potter, 1995.

Bliss, Anne. *A Handbook of Dyes from Natural Materials*. New York: Charles Scribner's Sons, 1981.

Boyd, Nancy Long. *The Pine Cone Book: Cones, Christmas and Recollections*. Baltimore, Md.: Prospect Hill, 1983.

Brown, John Hull. *Early American Beverages*. Rutland, Vt.: Charles E. Tuttle Company, 1966.

Brown, Margery. *The Complete Book of Rush and Basketry Techniques*. New York: Larousse & Co., Inc., 1983.

Brown, Tom, Jr. *Tom Brown's Field Guide to Living with the Earth.* New York: Berkley Books, 1984.

Brown, Vinson. *Reading the Woods: Seeing More in Nature's Familiar Faces*. New York: Collier Books, 1969.

Busch, Phyllis S. *Wildflowers and the Stories behind Their Names*. New York: Charles Scribner's Sons, 1977.

Clymer, R. Swinburne. *Nature's Healing Agents: Herbs, Roots and Barks and Their Use in the Prevention and Elimination of Disease*. 5th ed. Glenwood, Ill.: Meyerbooks, 1973.

Cooke, Viva and Julia Sampley. *Palmetto Braiding and Weaving*. Peoria, Ill.: Manual Arts Press, 1947.

*Many out-of-print books can be obtained from local libraries, book sales, and book-search organizations.

Creekmore, Betsey B. *Traditional American Crafts: A Practical Guide to 300 Years of Methods and Materials.* New York: Hearthside Press Inc., 1968.

Critchley, Paula. *The Art of Shellcraft.* New York: Praeger Publishers, 1975.

Cusick, Dawn and Carol Taylor. *Nature Crafts for Christmas: A Step-by-Step Guide to Making Wreaths, Ornaments & Decorations.* Emmaus, Penn.: Rodale Press, 1994.

Cvancara, Alan M. *A Field Manual for the Amateur Geologist: Tools and Activities for Exploring Our Planet.* New York: John Wiley & Sons, 1985, 1995.

Day, Jere and Linda Peavy. *The Complete Book of Rock Crafting.* New York: Drake Publishers, Inc., 1976.

Eastman, John. *The Book of Forest and Thicket: Trees, Shrubs, and Wildflowers of Eastern North America.* Harrisburg, Penn.: Stackpole Books, 1992.

Epple, Anne Orth. *Nature Crafts.* Radnor, Penn.: Chilton Book Company, 1974.

Erdmann, LaDora. *Driftwood Techniques and Projects.* New York: Drake Publishers, Inc., 1974.

Fenton, Carroll Lane, and Mildred Adams Fenton. *Riches from the Earth: The Story of Our Mineral Resources.* New York: John Day Company, 1953.

Fiarotta, Phyllis. *Snips & Snails & Walnut Whales: Nature Crafts for Children.* New York: Workman Publishing Company, 1975.

Fraser, Antonia. *A History of Toys.* New York: Delacorte Press, 1966.

Gamlin, Linda. *Trees.* New York: Dorling Kindersley, Inc., 1997.

Gillooly, Maryanne. *Natural Baskets.* Pownal, Vt.: Storey Communications, Inc., 1992.

Gould, Mary Earle. *The Early American House: Household Life in America 1620–1850.* Rutland, Vt.: Charles E. Tuttle Co., Inc., 1949, 1965.

———. *Early American Wooden Ware & Other Kitchen Utensils.* Rutland, Vt.: Charles E. Tuttle Co., Inc., 1962.

Hayes, M. Vincent. *Artistry in Wood—Ideas, History, Tools, Techniques: Carving, Sculpture, Assemblage, Woodcuts.* New York: Drake Publishers, Inc., 1972.

Hilger, Sister M. Inez. *Chippewa Child Life and Its Cultural Background.* St. Paul, Minn.: Minnesota Historical Society Press, 1951, 1992.

Hunt, W. Ben. *Ben Hunt's Big Book of Whittling.* New York: Bruce Publishing Company, 1944.

James, George Wharton. *Indian Blankets & Their Makers.* New York: Dover Publications, Inc., 1914, 1920, 1974.

Jones, Iris Sanderson. *Early North American Dollmaking: A Narrative History and Craft Instructions.* San Francisco: 101 Productions, 1976.

Kapoun, Robert W. *Language of the Robe: American Indian Trade Blankets.* Salt Lake City, Utah: Peregrine Smith Books, 1992.

Kavasch, Barrie. *Native Harvests: Recipes and Botanicals of the American Indian.* New York: Vintage Books, 1979.

Kohl, MaryAnn F. *Mudworks: Creative Clay, Dough, and Modeling Experiences.* Bellingham, Wash.: Bright Ring Publishing, 1989.

———, and Cindy Gainer. *Good Earth Art: Environmental Art for Kids.* Bellingham, Wash.: Bright Ring Publishing, 1991.

Kopper, Philip. *The Wild Edge: Life and Lore of the Great Atlantic Beaches.* Chester, Conn.: Globe Pequot Press, 1979, 1991.

Landsman, Anne Cheek. *Needlework Designs from the American Indians: Traditional Patterns of the Southeastern Tribes.* Cranbury, N.J.: A.S. Barnes and Company, Inc., 1977.

Laubin, Reginald, and Gladys Laubin. *American Indian Archery.* Norman, Okla.: University of Oklahoma Press, 1980.

Lingelbach, Jenepher, ed. *Hands-On Nature: Information and Activities for Exploring the Environment with Children.* Woodstock, Vt.: Vermont Institute of Natural Science, 1986.

Lohf, Sabine. *Nature Crafts.* Chicago: Children's Press, Inc., 1990.

MacFarlan, Allan A. *Living Like Indians: A Treasury of American Indian Crafts, Games and Activities.* New York: Bonanza Books, 1961.

Mason, Bernard S. *Crafts of the Woods.* South Brunswick: A.S. Barnes and Company, Inc., 1973.

Metcalf, Harlan G. *Whittlin', Whistles, and Thingamajigs: The Pioneer Book of Nature Crafts and Recreation Arts.* Harrisburg, Penn.: Stackpole Books, 1974.

Michael, Pamela. *All Good Things Around Us.* New York: Holt, Rinehart and Winston, 1980.

Miles, Bebe. *Designing with Natural Materials.* New York: Van Nostrand Reinhold Company, 1975.

Musselman, Virginia W. *Learning about Nature through Crafts.* Harrisburg, Penn.: Stackpole Books, 1969.

Phillips Petroleum Company. *Pasture and Range Plants.* Bartlesville, Okla.: Phillips Petroleum Company, 1963.

Plummer, Beverly. *Earth Presents: How to Make Beautiful Gifts from Nature's Bounty.* New York: Atheneum, 1974.

Robertson, Seonaid. *Dyes from Plants.* New York: Van Nostrand Reinhold Company, 1973.

Schneider, Richard C. *Crafts of the North American Indians: A Craftsman's Manual.* New York: Van Nostrand Reinhold Company, 1972.

Souter, Gillian. *Naturecrafts: 50 Extraordinary Gifts & Projects, Step by Step.* New York: Crown Trade Paperbacks, 1996.

Stapleton, Constance. *Crafts of America: A Guide to the Finest Traditional Crafts Made in the United States.* New York: Harper & Row, Publishers, 1988.

Tekiela, Stan, and Karen Shanberg. *Nature Smart: A Family Guide to Nature.* Cambridge, Minn.: Adventure Publications, 1995.

Thomas, Anne Wall. *Colors from the Earth.* New York: Van Nostrand Reinhold Company, 1980.

Thomas, David Hurst et al. *The Native Americans: An Illustrated History.* Atlanta: Turner Publishing, Inc., 1993.

Thorpe, Patricia. *Everlastings: The Complete Book of Dried Flowers.* New York: Quarto Marketing Ltd., 1985.

Van Rensselaer, Eleanor. *Decorating with Pods and Cones.* Princeton, N.J.: D. Van Nostrand Company, Inc., 1957.

Vitale, Alice Thoms. *Leaves in Myth, Magic & Medicine.* New York: Stewart, Tabori & Chang, 1997.

Wellford, Lin. *The Art of Painting Animals on Rocks.* Cincinnati, Ohio: North Light Books, 1994.

Westland, Pamela. *The Step by Step Art of Nature Crafts.* Secaucus, N.J.: Chartwell Books, Inc., 1994.

Wilbur, C. Keith. *Indian Handcrafts: How to Craft Dozens of Practical Objects Using Traditional Indian Techniques.* Old Saybrook, Conn.: Globe Pequot Press, 1990.

Do you have an idea for a naturally creative craft? Or have you created something unique out of natural raw materials? If so, the author would love to hear from you. Your craft might even be included in a future book. Jot your craft idea on a piece of paper or take a picture of a completed craft, along with a description of how you made it, and send it with your name, address, and daytime phone number to:

Amy E. Dean
c/o M. Evans and Company, Inc.
216 East 49th Street
New York, NY 10017

Index